The
Mystic
Way

The
Mystic
Way

The Seeker's Guide to Spiritual Journeying

Sara
Wiseman

Dedication

For those who seek to explore the Divine realms—portals of the Universe where the Mystery can be known—I am so pleased to offer this work. I am grateful to all of you, spiritual pioneers willing to explore and evolve.

Table of Contents

Preface

I've been journeying throughout the Universe since before I can remember.

If you've found this book, you probably have too.

When I was young, I didn't know that what I did was called journeying. Most of us didn't have a name for what we did. We just "went there," into these realms that other people called our "imagination." Except these places weren't imaginary at all. There were and are real—different dimensionalities that we can return to again and again, as real as any real life could be.

But when were young, we didn't have this understanding. Some of us were taught to hide this ability, and most of us were taught to mistrust it. Even now, as evolving humans, we were starting to own our own power—we're just starting to understand that the spiritual realms are real.

In ancient times, we were all mystics and shamans. But after thousands of years and so many changes in our world, we've simply forgotten that we can do this. It's only now that we are remembering, as a human collective, again.

In my own experience, it took a near-death experience in 2000 to help me remember my true nature once again, and to begin to piece together a vocabulary for what happens to me—and us all— when we "go there." It took many years before I finally began to understand how spiritual journeying really works—how to crack the code, so to speak, so that we can work in the realms in a repeatable, teachable way.

If you've found this book, you're in the process of remembering too.

In your own life, you've probably journeyed millions of times—but may not be sure how you do it. You've soul traveled all over the Universe—but you may not be sure of how you "get there," and how you get back.

By journeying, I mean traveling to the etheric realms in consciousness, as a soul experience. The places you visit might be called the etheric realms, the imaginal realms, the spirit world, the realms of guides and angels, the Akashic Records, the shamanic worlds, or something else. We journey to many places and dimensions we don't have names for yet.

And yet, what's interesting is this: when we journey—when we soul travel—we often or even always visit the same places, or the same kinds of places. We visit the same portals, we use the same systems to travel, we understand soul language the same way.

There is commonality in our experience.

And just as with a physical trip on the earth plane, our soul travel is consistent—it is a repeatable process that we can learn to do at will. It is a process that we can learn and that we can teach to others.

Which is why I am so pleased to offer this book as a guide, a map, a wayshower to take you to common, collective dimensions we visit when we journey—to show you how to get there and how to get back, so that you can explore for yourself.

In this book, I will introduce you to all the places I go and have been going to for my whole life, and show you how I get there. There are places that will be familiar to you, because they are the places that all souls travel to, over and over again. Again, these places have different names: heaven, the angelic realms, the guide realms, the Akashic Records, the lower, middle and upper worlds, the Tree of Life, past lives and future lives, to list a few.

But the names don't matter, not really.

What's important is what happens to you when you are there—what you learn as a soul.

As you read this book, you will learn what to expect as you visit each Divine portal—what or who you might encounter, how to proceed in different situations, and most importantly, how to receive the Divine guidance and healing that is always waiting for us, whenever we journey in the unlimited consciousness of the Universe.

Let us journey together.

The Universe awaits.

Introduction

When you close your eyes, where do you go?

When you meditate, where are you?

When you zone out while driving, showering or doing some mindless task, what happens?

Where do you exist when you fall into a memory, or when you find yourself in reverie in nature, or when you dream?

All of these experiences are ways we journey into the etheric realms without even knowing we are journeying—we slip behind the veil before we are aware it's even happening, and then we exist there—in this other reality, this etheric realm—for some time.

In earth time, we might be there a few seconds, a few minutes.

But in etheric time, time is not linear.

It is experiential.

It is only beingness, outside of time.

So that a minute in meditation may seem like an hour. Or vice versa.

And yet we know we exist there, because when we are there, we have experiences that are real—that connect with and influence and inform us about the relationships, experiences and events in our "real" life. When we journey in the etheric realms, we have understandings, feelings, healings. We receive visions that contain symbolic information that relate to our "real" lives now or to our "real" lives in many lifetimes. We foresee and foreknow, both what has already happened, and what we couldn't possibly know yet.

Most of all, when we journey we come into a place or space of grace, where all things are experienced as wholeness, love and light.

In the etheric realms, we find nourishment—Divine sustenance and healing—that helps us find the answers to all our questions, and to understand ourselves our souls. And when we experience ourselves as souls—not egos or bodies—this changes us when we return to our human reality, our earth life.

Even just a few seconds of soul work can change us permanently.

We come back from our journeying different than we were before: less petty, less cranky, less confused, less afraid. We come back as our soul selves.

And every time we immerse ourselves in this luminous, higher vibration reality, we come back changed and changed again.

Divine portals

Where we go in the etheric realms isn't random—we just don't disappear into our souls without direction or destination. In fact, what I have discovered in teaching this style of journeying to so many students for so many years, is that we consistently go to the same places—the same portals, the same dimensions, the same vibrational areas—every single time we enter in.

And, we do not return to the same places ourselves, but we return to the same places as each other, over and over again. In other words, we journey into Universal mind. The place we go is to ourselves, as One soul.

I find this incredibly exciting!

That we, as humans, continually show up into the same places when we journey—not because we are told to go there, or directed to go there, or even because we think we will go there, but because we go there because we already know the way.

We are souls, heading once again for our soul home.

And, to be perfectly clear about my approach and what I teach:

I am not taking about religion's heaven.

I am not talking about psychology's subconscious.

I am not talking about science's brain chemistry or quantum physics or string theory or God particle.

I teach the mystic way—a method of communing with the Universe in direct connection, using a light meditative or trance state. As a mystic, you will journey into the etheric realms, and discover what happens as you explore. This is an experiential path, and frankly, there are not a lot of markers along the way.

Over the centuries, many teachers have explored these realms, each from their own perspective or from the perspective of their field of study. Yet, the realms as a whole are not well documented in modern times. They come to us as a tradition, in religious mysticism or ancient shamanistic practices, or more recently as new age practices.

In all times—old and new—this path has not been and is not now mainstream.

Which, of course, makes it all the more interesting to explore!

For example, in one of my past lives, I was a French-Canadian trapper, making my way from east to west along the borderline of Canada and the U.S. The terrain was all wilderness, and I was very much on my own, now and then stopping at trading posts to share stories with fellow trappers and traders. In that lifetime, I was an explorer in the extreme.

I feel the same now. Except this time, of course, I am not traveling the wilderness of nature. I am exploring the wild, uncharted territory of our One soul and—if you are reading this— where it is now or in many years in the future, we are making this journey together.

Don't worry too much if the mainstream doesn't understand your path. We are the pioneers, early to the path. And oh, the wisdom there to be discovered! The Mystery, for those who dare to travel the uncharted path, and head into new spiritual territory!

To follow the mystic way is to allow yourself to have direct connection, to surrender deeply to the infinite mystery, and to experience yourself, over and over again, as soul. As you do this, you will gain the unshakeable understanding that we are One.

You will understand that we are infinite.

That consciousness never dies.

That nothing is separate.

When you understand this—not as theory or rhetoric, but from your own visceral and true experience—your life is changed forever.

In this book, we'll travel to all the portals, places and spaces that I have visited with my students for many years. We'll come back to these same portals, because this is where we are journeying as collective soul. And we'll make the pilgrimage again and again, so we can know ourselves as souls again.

How to use this book

This book will teach you how to journey in the etheric realms—it is a guide and a map to all you will experience. It will teach you the common portals we visit as collective soul, and how to access Universal wisdom sources that will help you understand yourself and the karma of your life. We'll work with guides and angels, karma, the Akashic Records, and past and future lives. All, with the goal of understanding ourselves better—as humans living on earth—and as souls who exist in infinite connection.

You'll learn through teaching, exercises, meditations and journaling—and always, we will work in tandem with the Universe, for there is no time we are not supported and guided, no matter if we believe this or not. At the end of this book, you will also find the eight questions the Universe most wants you to ask—these questions designed to be answered with assistance from the guides and angels, and can be returned to again and again.

Finally, there is no special gift or ability required to do this work. You don't need to have a meditation practice, or follow a religion, or have a certain belief system, or have been to workshops or done training. Just show up with beginner's mind, with a sense of curiosity and interest, and see what happens.

I've taught the mystic way—spiritual journeying—to a great many people for a very long time, and I know without doubt that the Universe will take you to exactly where you need to go.

Part One

Journeying

Lesson 1

Unexpected Journeying

Last night, I was awakened from a deep, dreaming sleep by a loud explosion in my left ear. It sounded like a bomb had gone off, right on my pillow. It was a massive, loud, cracking boom, and I sat up in terror and confusion, trying to get my bearings. In my panic, I was certain something important had just happened, or that I had just received the sign that something very important would happen soon.

Fearfully, I called upon my angels—not in the calm, meditative way I normally work in the etheric realms—but as a true calling out. Whenever I feel I am in danger, I immediately revert to my earliest sources of comfort: I call upon God, I call upon the angelic realm, I call on all the forces of Light to assist me in my distress.

They arrived in legion, filling the room, and as I sensed the energy shift from fear to safety, I started to check in with each of my family members, soul to soul, to make sure everyone was okay. All of them were sleeping, and I connected with them easily. All accounted for, all safe, no one in danger, everyone still in the land of the living and light.

With everyone accounted for, I relaxed in the dark room. I rested my back against the headboard of the bed, and wondered why I had been awakened in this abrupt, shocking way.

Science has a name for this experience: exploding head syndrome. For some people it happens frequently, at that moment between waking and sleeping, or in the middle of a deep sleep. For others, it happens once in a lifetime, or during times of extreme stress. It's benign, there's no cure. It's one of those things we don't understand, and maybe won't understand for a long time.

The brain, such a great mystery.

But the soul, an even greater mystery still.

Because this experience may, or may not, be merely physiological. It may be instead be spiritual. I have had this experience several times, but only since I've been actively exploring the astral realms. Other psychics and seers have likened it to a sonic boom—the loud crash of sound waves or energy waves that is created when a jet moves from one level of speed to another.

In other words, it is a sound that happens when we break through a barrier. Which is exactly what do when we travel in the liminal realms—when we shift from earth reality to spiritual reality. We break through a barrier. We cross the veil.

After the "boom" experience, I fell back asleep, and spent the whole night traveling, traveling, traveling in all kinds of realms. We all do this—sleep is rest for the earth body only, but it is the time the soul is truly alive to travel, work and explore.

When I woke it was morning, and I reflected on the angels who'd been in the room, and the sun streaming in my window, and the loud explosion that I'd experienced.

My own way of looking at things is not skewed to the scientific or psychological—at least not as my first take. My first take is spiritual and intuitive—it's how I see the world.

It isn't that I don't value science and psychology—I do. I feel the scientific fields are absolutely related to the work of the spiritual and intuitive realms. Scientists, doctors, psychics, shamans—we are all exploring the Mystery from different sides of the equation. So, too, are people working in the creative fields, or in anything that involves curiosity and compassion and evolution. Whenever we seek to understand Oneness, in all the ways it can be understood, this is what we are doing.

So my take is that this loud explosion—this violent overwhelming jolt of energy—is some kind of energy "boom" or pop that happens when I am going from being asleep in my earth bed, to when I am breaking into an out-of-body experience.

It is the moment the switch happens from soul in human body to soul on the astral plane.

Most of us astral project—we go out of body—every single time we sleep. Our body stays safe and secure in our beds, waiting for us to return, while our souls slips out the window to go play and work and explore in the astral realms.

We astral project—we go out of body—when we dream our small or scattered dreams that don't make sense, when we have meaningful dreams, when we have nightmares, and when we have what I call prophetic or visionary dreams—big dreams that guide us to our destiny. We'll discuss those more later.

When we astral project—when we go into the astral realms— at the moment we shift dimensions from earth to soul reality, there is an energy exchange. Thus, the explosion I heard. The great booming thunder of energy shifting, or barriers being broken through.

It is, of course, what happens is not always this big. In fact, we often astral project with no energy boom at all. This is what interests me—why on that particular night, as I switched from human reality to soul reality, as I went out of body—why that was a bigger shift than on other nights. Did I travel further? Did I travel to new realms? Did something else happen?

I don't remember my dreams that night. If I did, perhaps they would hold clues to what this big "boom" was about, or perhaps not. The bigger sense I have is that while I am in the process of writing this, my focus is on this—the long-held desire to explore and share the portals and dimensions and places I go, so that others may also go there. This intention, this desire to go forth, see and share, may be enhancing or accelerating my experiences. We shall see.

For now, we can just understand that we are shifting realms all the time. When we sleep, when we meditate, whenever we trance out. All the time.

In fact, the question might be more apropos: when are we really fully in human reality? It seems to me, we exist more fully, more infinitely and more eternally, on the soul plane.

Liminal states

We journey to the other realms accidentally—when we don't hold intention to do so—in many different ways. We go into a liminal state—we are on the edge, at the limit of what our "real life" consciousness tells us, and at the edge of another state.

Sometimes this feels like falling off the edge of the world. One moment we are "here," and the next we are somewhere else entirely, and we have no idea how we got there. We have accidentally journeyed—gone to another state of consciousness entirely.

This can happen in an accident, such as a car accident—we might simply disassociate from the shock, and have no idea where we've gone and been.

And yet, most times, there is no accident about it. Our daily lives are filled with unintentional journeying. In fact, of all the hours in our 24-hour day, it might be noted that we spend more time in the etheric realms, than in the "real world."

This means that journeying—even when it is entirely unexpected—is not rare, infrequent, casual or special. It is how we are designed, and it is who we are. The soul cannot be kept from the Universe, because it is the Universe. Thus, we cannot be disconnected from what we are. We are always in communication with our own Source. The "real world" tries to tell us otherwise but, of course, this is not "real," or rather, it is not any more real than the etheric world.

We might compare "real" life as we experience it as a shared dream that we are all dreaming together—a shared reality that we agree on. Or it might not be a dream, it might be a dimension. The key is this: there are many realities, many dimensions, many dreams.

As souls, we inhabit many worlds at once—we continually exist in the liminal states.

Sleeping

Consider what happens when we sleep—we tuck our bodies away into a safe place, or a place that feels safe at the moment, and then we let go of our awareness. We drop into "somewhere else," for hours and hours—nearly one third of our day.

Nobody thinks it's weird, because we all do it.

So why does it seem weird to think or talk about?

We suspend our awareness, and we do so willingly. We don't know how we do it either—we just do it. In fact, if sleep weren't so common, so much a part of our experience, we would certainly find it unusual—that we just "check out" for such a long period of time each night, every night.

Animals sleep, of course, but do trees sleep? Do stones sleep? We don't really know. What we do know is that we, as humans, periodically and consistently suspend ourselves in a different reality—we shut down our awareness, and our consciousness goes somewhere else. We don't plan on it, we don't try to, we just "go there" to this somewhere else all of a sudden, without knowing that we were going there, or how we were going to get there. Sometimes, we aren't even cognizant that we are in another realm, or we don't know this until later on.

So, where do we go when we sleep? Do we go into dreamland, and if so where is that? What, exactly, is "dreamland"? Do we go somewhere else, to the land of spirits? Do we go somewhere else, into the etheric realms? We go all those places, every night—and we have no idea how we get there or where we are.

When I was young, I used to love a fairy tale called *The 12 Dancing Princesses*. In it, 12 sisters are locked in their castle each night—yet each night they escape! They row boats across a river to a magical island where they dance all night, only to return to "real" life at dawn, with their slippers worn to shreds. Their "real" life is in the castle, during the day. But isn't their magical life at night, on the astral plane, just as real? Isn't their dream dancing just as real, with shredded slippers as proof?

This is what sleeping is like. We tuck our body into a still state, arranging it so it will be comfortable and warm until we return. And then we astral project, visiting hither and thon, until it is time to come home at dawn. Whether we remember our "dreams" or not, we have certainly been away. Only our bodies have been here.

And yet, sleeping is not the only way we unexpectedly "go there." Other unexpected journeys are also common experiences, including:

- Déjà vu
- Disassociation
- Beingness
- Daydreaming
- Dreaming
- Trance
- Reverie

Sometimes they are more dramatic, such as:

- Astral travel
- Peak experiences
- Transcendent sex
- Near accident
- Near death experience

⊙ Spiritual awakening
⊙ Death

What all of these states have in common is a kind of slipping beyond the veil—it is a momentary release of this dream of "real" life, and an entering into another dream, in the etheric realm. We'll talk more about where we go later. For now, let's look at the method of transport: how is it that we "go there" so easily and so often?

In a nutshell, the bridge is Nowness.

Any time we become conscious in the moment, we begin to exist in Now. When we are in this state of beingness, we exist out of space and time—or rather, we exist in all space and all time at once. This condition of existing outside of space and time is exactly the condition of being that lets us easily slip "beyond the veil" into another dimension.

You've probably experienced most, if not all, of the liminal states. Let's take a look at each in turn:

Déjà vu

Déjà vu is having the sense of having experienced something before. We "know" it, whether it is a place, a feeling, a person, an object, or even a scent or atmosphere. It is familiar. We have the sense that this is not our first time having this experience, and indeed, it is most likely not. As souls, we travel in different dimensions of time and space all the time. When we dream or otherwise enter different realities in this lifetime, we find ourselves in past or future lifetimes. When we exist in past or future lifetimes, we often visit this lifetime. We are continually experiences we've had or will have, like time travelers continually dropping into the unlimited lifetimes we have as soul. When we journey intentionally, this also happens. It is no wonder so many things, places, people and experiences are familiar. We have indeed seen it all before.

When you fall into déjà vu, you fall into another dimension of time. Again, liminal states have a feeling of falling off the edge. You might end up in the past or the future. When you fall into déjà vu, you enter another time.

I lived part of my childhood in Europe, and in these places teeming with history, this was a frequent experience. We would visit an ancient building—a castle, an historical part of town, a ruin of some kind—and I would know I had been there before. Sometimes, the present scene would fade away, and I would see what had happened long ago, taking place in front of me—there would be people cooking in the castle kitchen, or children playing in the hallways, or guards at the guard house, or priests in the church, whatever it was—I would transport to a real where I could see that life in front of me, as if I were a fly on the wall.

Other times, I could not see the past scene as clearly, but I could still sense something—I felt the familiarity, as if I'd been there so many times. It was a kind of familiarity or sentimentality—this emotional connection and knowing of what had happened in other times, experienced as part of this time.

I am positive that you have had these kinds of experiences too, in all kinds of places far and near.

Déjà vu is a portal that lead us to time travel, but we only reach the doorway. We stand in the doorway, and we sense that odd, shifting, confusing, tingly feeling of déjà vu and we might even say aloud "I'm having déjà vu." But we are still in the doorway, at the entrance to the portal. We may continue journeying and go through, or we may not.

Dreaming

Ah, the dream world. When I was younger I was a tremendous sleeper, but now that I am older, I wake many nights at the time of the *amrit vela*. I am awakened to channel, to meditate, or because of the intensity of my dreams. It has gotten so that I have detached from the expectation of the solid eight sleep hours of my youth, because I know this is not my purpose now—I am called to astral travel far and wide, every night.

We all dream, and we soul travel all over the Universe when we dream. We astral project; our consciousness travels. Again, this is an example of unexpected traveling: for the most part we don't know how to do it, save for getting in bed and closing our eyes and allowing ourselves to "drift off" into sleep.

We put on our warm blankets, a way of tucking the body in safely, and we allow our souls to drift out of human container.

We usually can't direct where we go, although sometimes if we hold intention in the moments before we fall asleep we can. What happens—where we go when we dream—is always surprising. We journey to places we know well, and to places we've never been, and to places we can't imagine. We don't try to go there. We just do.

In dreaming, we visit different places, but even more so, we visit different dimensions and different times, and we often visit places that are parallel but different to our "real" life. Certainly, our dreams are ways we work out our emotions, and often, our dreams are prophetic or even warning. When we wake up with a very strong dream, and then elements of that dream happen in our real life, we are guided to pay attention to what is happening, symbolically, emotionally and archetypally—we are learning to speak the language of the Universe.

Dreaming happens when we sleep. Some people say they can control their dreams, and I believe it is possible to control some of what we dream. We can set intention to have peaceful or healing dreams, for example. Or you can visit spiritual teachers who teach in the astral planes—you can set intention when you are falling asleep to go to these astral classrooms, and when you go there, you will learn a great many things about the spirit world. In my own dreams, I am there a lot. I do not request to go there, I just do, and I also experience "graduation" ceremonies where I am told that I have mastered some new understanding about being a soul.

I am not special. We all have these experiences. We all go to these spirit schools when we dream. We all receive Divine guidance when we dream.

Interestingly, we don't just dream as individuals. We also dream as collective soul. We enter the river or stream of all souls, and we experience what all souls are experiencing, all together. This is where vivid dreams happen, where there is a great deal of intensity—so much intensity we might label it as a nightmare. When we enter the stream of collective soul, of collective consciousness, we process with everyone else, all that is happening in our "real" life. We will often deal with the soul lessons we are all collectively learning as part of human evolution.

For example, many people will have dreams of natural disasters, such as hurricanes, fires or earthquakes before they happen, and in the days following. They are tapping into the great well of collective suffering that we are experience together, as we feel each other's suffering with compassion and empathy. How can we prevent this suffering? This is a question we are working on as soul collective now—we are learning to transcend suffering.

Sometimes we unintentionally drop into astral realms in more dramatic ways, such as during these circumstances.

Astral projection

Astral projection is something that happens to many people, where they leave their earth body and inhabit an astral body. In this astral body, they travel the Universe. There is lots of information about astral travel out there, especially the phenomenon of sleep paralysis and the buzzing and vibration that people experience at the moment of departure and reentry into the earth body. I would love to write about this, but I have not had that experience: I do not travel in an astral body, I travel as a point of consciousness.

If you are traveling in an astral body, it can be very interesting to work with that and explore what happens. If you are traveling as a point of consciousness, this is interesting too.

I believe I travel without an astral body, or without the awareness of the astral body, because I have spent so many years working in third eye, that this is a more natural way for me to travel in the astral realms. We are all different, some of us more associated with the chakras, the subtle bodies, others of us more associated with clairvoyance, channeling. We each bring our abilities as part of the whole.

Disassociating

Disassociating is a way we go elsewhere, to escape where we are. Because disassociating is a psychological term, I also use the more colloquial terms of spacing out or blanking out. Spacing out happens frequently when we are bored, or when we find our situation unpleasant or without interest. We just space out, and we go somewhere else. Kids and teens do this all the time, but many adults also have kept the trick of looking like they are paying attention to one thing, when they are really somewhere else entirely. Spacing out has some other similar states, which might include blanking out, which is when we just go somewhere else during physically activity, music or art. For example, when I ride my bike, there is a certain hill where I often blank out; I just go somewhere else when I go downhill. I sometimes can't remember if I've ridden the hill or not, even a few minutes after I've done it. Another similar and more extreme way of spacing out is disassociating, which is the trick everyone who's experienced emotional, physical or sexual abuse or any kind of trauma knows well—we disassociate during harmful experience. We go elsewhere. Our bodies are in the room, but our souls have fled to safer grounds. Sometimes, we disassociate so fully that we have trouble calling our soul back in. But in most cases, disassociation is beneficial soul travel—it protects us from the unbearable.

Daydreaming

Daydreaming is similar to spacing out, except it is a more complete journey. We find ourselves one moment sitting in a classroom staring out the window, and then next we are in fantasy or in the imaginal realm. We are "thinking" about other things, and these seem to take on a life of their own, so that they become more important than the "real" life classroom scene we are in. What is interesting about daydreaming, is that it tends to show us creative answers, it tends to show us what we long for, and it tends to show us our truth. For example, if you don't like your job, you may find yourself daydreaming about a new job. Your daydream will help you understand your heart's longing. If you continue long enough with that daydream or allow yourself to have this daydream frequently, you may be shown what this job looks like, how to get it, and what you will feel when you get it. All of this aspect of daydreaming is a way we work out our problems and receive guidance, even though it appears we are simply existing in our real world situation.

Beingness

Beingness is way of becoming so attuned to everything all at once, we discover ourselves in a bliss state of Nowness. People who have achieved a high level of consciousness exist in beingness—they experience connection love, light and everything all at once, in all or in most moments. Beingness is where our soul journey is taking us—to learn how to exist in this enlightened state all the time. **Flow** is a symptom of beingness—when we are in flow, we are in a state of absolute unified awareness of everything all at once that lets us notice and follow the signs of the Universe perfectly, without hesitation or second guessing. Flow is absolute intuition, instantly acted upon. Flow is the trance of beingness that allows the Universe to guide us at a soul level.

Trance

Trance can happen intentionally, in meditation for example, but it also just happens. For example, when we drive, bike, dance, run or walk we often go into trance—there is something about the body moving through space and time that shifts our reality. When we swim, take a shower or bath we often go into trance—there is something about immersion in water that takes us there. Trance also happens during drumming or other rhythmic or tonal activities, when there are rhythmic patterns that we attach to. Many people experience trance channeling and psychic abilities when they do something as simple as drumming or play music—the rhythm and vibration are a bridge to the other world.

For example, this afternoon I went on a bike ride in the woods, and within a few moments I found myself in a state of trance. For me, bike riding is a physical experience—I have to pedal and navigate and balance and use energy—and yet it's also, without fail, a spiritual experience. The trails wind, the trees canopy everything, birds flock, and I propel through time and space and am open to the wind and the trees and everything. After the first few pedals, it's all a blur. The trance happens that quickly.

It's not that I'm not aware: each part of the path is known to me as I ride—I can remember what the grasses look like by the pond, and how the open spaces are dry and sparse and hum with crickets, how the trail through the orchards smells of blackberries. I can tell you if the river is high or low, and if there are "vees" of geese flying, or an eagle soaring. I can tell you if the bees are active or sleepy. I can tell you if a bunny darts across the path, or even if something bigger rustles in the brush nearby.

I can tell you all that, and yet I am fully in beingness—again that word, reverie. A part of me goes away as I am riding—I am no longer the person with worldly concerns, or the person with thoughts, or the person with worries. A part of me—the "real" life me—dies. I enter into a different realm. I dissolve into everything and nothing and become pure consciousness.

I do not know how I entered this state while biking, and I do not really remember what happened or happens when I am in that space. I start pedaling, and I enter a spiritual portal, unintentionally. The act is unintentional and often takes me by surprise, and yet I can repeat the experience—all I have to do is go on another bike ride, and it will simply "happen" again. I will just "go there." Still, I don't know how my consciousness shifts. In biking, for example, I am aware that there are certain conditions— nature, movement, rhythm—and yet, why do I "go there" during some parts of a bike ride and not others? I am not aware of my trance in the portal until after it is over. I enter the portal, and my identity and thoughts and mind are no longer here. Just as when I sleep, I enter a suspended state, where my consciousness exists elsewhere. I don't know I've "been there" until I am back in this world.

Reverie

Reverie is another aspect of trance, and arrives when we experience beauty. It is a state of bliss when we come across something so harmonic, we are catapulted to an enlightened state. We fall into a state of reverie, which is a state of love. Great art and music bring us to reverie; we become enchanted by harmony and wholeness.

Peak experiences

Peak experiences are moments so "big" we can't believe they're real. We're in a heightened state of bliss, joy or gratitude. This can happen when you finally achieve a long-held goal, such as running a marathon. During the marathon, you will experience many emotions: pain, excitement, confusion, nirvana and much more. All of this may culminate in a feeling of over-the-top joy when you finally cross the finish line—you may have a sense that everything is euphoric at this moment—so much so that you don't exist in space or time. You dissolve. Kundalini opening is a kind of peak experience that is felt in the energy body. Kundalini experiences said to be infrequent, even once in a lifetime, but in truth they happen to us all the time—if you have had one, you instantly recognize the way energy moves up your spine to your crown chakra, and the peak experience this brings of dissolving into everything.

Transcendent sex

Transcendent sex is another dream state that is a trance of connection with another person. Along with birth, sex is the closest way we can be with another human—it is a way of merging body and communing soul. When we are in transcendent sex, we may have the sense of spontaneously flipping into past lives or future lives, of shifting environments so we don't know where we are, of entering trance, of having kundalini awakening, and of a state of complete beingness. It is no mistake that the act of creation is so sacred, whether it is used for reproduction or for connection.

When we experience transcendent sex, we go somewhere else—we journey into another dimensionality. Some call orgasm "la petite mort" which translates from French as "the little death." It is an expression that describes a brief loss or weakening of consciousness. And yet, it is not a loss of consciousness, because consciousness never changes. It is rather a shifting of our recognition of time and space in that moment. Orgasm alone does not create this portal; sexual transcendence is a spiritual opening, not a physical one.

A near accident

A near accident instantly jolts us into a state of awareness. It is a call back to the here and now. This does not mean it is a call back into "real" life, but rather into the reality of the soul. For example, the other day my husband and I were driving on a back road, and a car swooped around a curve and nearly hit us. We were not driving fast, it was not a dangerous street, and then this thing happened—the car swerved, we existed in the moment as the car headed toward us, and then in the last second, the car missed us. The driver kept going, oblivious to this close call. During this moment, my awareness was instantly shifted. My physical body was shaking, but my emotional self was transported into gratitude—I was reminded to see this life as a precious gift.

As another example, I was recently riding my bike as I often do, and I was in deep reverie from the trees, the wind, the light—I was in trance state. Then, unexpectedly, I was stung by a wasp on my ankle. It's not the same as a car accident, but it really shocked me and took me by surprise. I felt the sharp radiating pain on my ankle, and immediately I "went" somewhere else—my adrenaline kicked in and I just "left." In those minutes of heightened awareness, I was definitely between realms. I did not think or feel, and even now I can't remember what happened—I disassociated. The near accident was a moment that obliterated all other reality and took me completely into Nowness.

I did not feel a sense of gratitude for the wasp! But most certainly was shocked back into a Now state. When I look at what that Now state was, it's shocking. "I" wasn't there. Instead, everything was energy. I was not aware of "tree" or "path" or "bike" or even "body." I was mildly aware of a sound that was my own self yelling! But in general, everything was a blur. There was no time. I did not exist as "me" but only as consciousness, aware of pain. I did not even notice I had a body, for a few minutes. It was just energy, vibration, timelessness, consciousness. All that from a wasp sting!

And from what I have experienced, this is how it is when we are untethered soul—when we are truly in Nowness. When you are completely present, even if it happens because of something as common as a close call or a bug bite, you slip into the etheric realms without even knowing you are going there. You are jolted into understanding who you really are—not body or person, but consciousness in a shimmering, vibrating Universe of energy.

A near death experience

A near death experience is one of the most common ways to experience spiritual opening. One moment you are in your regular life. The next moment, you almost die—and you instantly experience the Universe/God/One/All and you know yourself as a soul. Different people have different experiences: they see themselves on an operating table, they see a tunnel of light, they see heaven, they see departed loved ones. Many people's experience (including my own) do not contain these elements. Instead, there is the knowing of "I am going to die" and then the peace that arrives in this moment when it is clear there is nothing to do, and the realization in the moment that consciousness can never be erased. And then, when you don't die (because near death by definition means you escape death) this understanding is with you. No matter what you thought before about death, the afterlife, heaven—you have now experienced it. This type of unexpected journeying is a way for the Universe to instantly upgrade us into higher levels of spiritual understanding.

A spiritual awakening

A spiritual awakening is a state of awakening that may begin in an instant, but then continues—you open and open and open further over time. You don't stop opening and expanding. This is where most of you reading this book are—you are in a state of continual expansion, and you have awareness that you are awakening.

Spiritual awakening might start with any unexpected journey that wakes us up from "real" life, and reminds us of our true reality as souls. The simplest things can open us, and this opening will continue. The light switch is turned on! We can't return to the dark! And so, we begin a process of waking up, waking up more, waking up more. This state of spiritual awakening can be subtle—we can realize we are changing, and over the next years we change and expand greatly. Or it can be dramatic—we wake up, and our entire life is changed forever.

For example, with my own spiritual awakening (triggered by a near-death experience which I've written about quite a bit, so I won't go into detail here), everything happened all at once—I became psychically open, I began to channel, and my spiritual understanding increased, all the while that my "real" life world disintegrated. Spiritual awakening is no small thing, and it often marks the ending of one stage of "real" life and the beginning of an entirely new, spiritually focused life. Finally, spiritual awakening is the journey of every soul. We all start this journey, at some point in our life. There is no time we as souls, are not journeying toward greater expansion.

Death

Death is the ultimate, unexpected portal. Robert Frost exhorted readers "to not go gently into that good night," and part of what his poem said was true: it is a good night, a shift from consciousness to consciousness as the soul drifts from the body. Yet, what he did not know, or did not believe, was that death was gentle.

To most of us, death seems very dramatic, but our experience of death at the time of death—the moments before or the moments of—may be not dramatic at all. It may be the gentlest of journeys, the unexpected slipping away of earth consciousness into etheric consciousness, the soul drifting from the body. I have not died in this lifetime yet, but I left my body so many times that I know that doing so is not painful, it does not hurt. In fact, it is a very peaceful experience.

And, consciousness does not end when we die.

Consciousness continues, whether we are alive or dead—there is no gap. It's always consciousness. This is because consciousness—the soul—simply is. It exists beyond the human body or the human brain. One minute we are in a body, and one minute we are out of body. Consciousness, the soul reality, does not change in this transition.

Certainly, when we have journeyed may times in the etheric realms—unexpectedly or intentionally—death becomes more familiar. Every time we head into the etheric realms—again, whether this just happens or we do it on purpose—we practice releasing and letting go into the infinite Now. We get used to it, we practice it. The more frequently we intentionally journey, meditate, pray and connect to the higher consciousness of God/One/All/Divine/Universe, the more we understand that all is love, and that there is nothing to fear.

If we are healthy and reasonably happy, we don't want to die. In fact, we avoid it as much as we can. And yet, in unexpected moments, death happens—the moment we shift from alive to dead, from consciousness to more consciousness—we don't have awareness of that moment of shifting. It's just more consciousness, but in a different realm.

Thus, death is yet another in a long list of experiences in which we unintentionally and unexpectedly shift into the etheric realms. We don't know how to get there. We aren't trying to get there. But we go there just the same.

Lesson 2

Intentional Journeying

We already know that we go places even when we aren't trying to. We journey, we astral travel, we find ourselves in different times and dimensions whenever we daydream, dream, die and all of the other various ways we journey without trying to journey.

We've looked at the ways we can unexpectedly journey.

Now, let's take a look at *intentional journeying*—the practice of entering into other times, dimensions and realms by intentionally going there.

All of us can do this.

It's not hard—it's easy.

In fact, it's ridiculously easy, because this is who we are. We're conscious, infinite souls who are always journeying—there isn't any time we're not existing in all dimensions at once. And yet, for one brief moment—this moment we call a lifetime—we try to ground outside into a human body, and contain ourselves within the confines of a human mind (a very small and limited container indeed!).

But of course, we are so much more than our body or mind.

We are so tremendously more expanded than this.

And the thing is—we don't have to try to be expanded. It's just who we are.

There is the idea in new age work of "remembering who you are" or "remembering your true self" as the secret to accessing this expanded nature that is you. That is a good way to think about it. There is also the idea shedding the layers of who you are not, and I have taught many times on the idea of letting go of and releasing all the Misbeliefs we've been raised with and continue to engage with.

Once you decide you want to—and this intentionality is the key—it is very easy to exist as consciousness only, without being limited by body or mind. You can do this right now if you want to. Anyone can.

You can, right now, simply close your eyes, relax, breath and "go there."

You can enter in, at will, to the other realms.

However, most people don't believe this is possible.

So, we have to trick the body and mind a little bit into relaxing.

We have to trick the body and mind to get out of the way.

In traditional meditation practices, one way this happens is by paying attention to the breath—the body and mind pay attention to the breath, and thus the soul is left unbothered to explore.

Other ways we might do this in traditional practice might be using a mantra, the repetition of sacred words. Or by practicing mudra, the repetition of particular hand movements.

And of course, there are many other practices—and if we take a look at the commonalities of those practices, we see that many or even most of them involve concentrating on something else, keeping the mind or the body or both busy at a particular task—so the soul can roam free.

If you're familiar with how I work, you already know that I don't teach traditional meditation practices, at least not in a traditional way! I only teach what I have experienced myself—even if I stumbled across that learning in an unexpected way. My practice is that I learn from what I experience, and then I will repeat the practice until I fully understand how it works on an experiential level, and when I finally get it, I will share it.

For the last twenty years, I've taught tens of thousands of people journeying—how to access the portals of consciousness where we commonly go as collective soul.

However, unlike traditional practices, I don't use the breath, or mantra or mudra as bridges or key entry points to this state. I think the breath, mantra and mudra are all very good bridges, it's just not how I stumbled upon my own experience.

So, I teach what I have experienced in my own mystic journey.

How I do things may or may not be the best way for you, but it is a method that's shown itself to be very easy for people with a modern, westernized mind to use. It's also very easy for children and teens to use.

After all, "going there" is not something foreign to us. It's something we do all day long. We are simply practicing remembering how it all works.

Also, this is not to say this practice wouldn't work for a non-westernized mind, or for a mind that has not been exposed to modern technologies. However, it is exceptionally simple for modern people to use, because it is so close to our everyday experience.

Why is this so? Let's take a look at our human experience, and how our "real life" has been evolving.

Evolution

Humans are changing beings. We not only are getting taller and bigger over the generations, but the way our minds work is also changing. At the time of this writing, most of us now living have experienced the industrial age, and now find ourselves fully immersed in the information age, and we have already begun to enter the intelligence age—artificial intelligence. Depending on how old you are, you either remember when computers, internet and smart devices came into your life—or if you are younger, you can't remember a time they didn't exist.

This is new for humanity.

It represents a lot of growth for the human body and mind.

There is a particular intuitivism to the way we search and access information from computers, and this not only mirrors the human mind, but it also teaches the human mind to work in that way. Everyone on earth right now who is using a computer or smart device, has become accustomed to this way of thinking.

It's intuitive, because it's search oriented—it moves from general to specific, vast to small. It's intuitive, because it seeks patterns and associations.

You might also say, the way we use technology now mirrors how we experience intuition: a search, using a computer screen, the way we go deeper into a search, even the way we understand how to play some video games. General to specific, vast to small.

It didn't used to be this way.

Our minds used to think differently.

Our journeying in books and movies was once a very long, meandering process. We read a book slowly, and experienced the insights of the author over time. It was a long, linear and either logical or narrative process. We watched a movie and the movie took a very long time to build, it took a long time to establish the characters, it took a long time to understand the plot.

Now, it is different. We might read a book on our phones, skimming to the parts that interest and skipping the rest. We might binge watch a series quickly, over the course of a weekend, so that an entire plotline for a season is provided in a few hours. What we watch is also different—no one bats an eye if a character is transported into a past life or alternate reality or works with not-yet-invented technology or converses with other beings. It is all part of what is in our collective consciousness now.

Indeed, many of us have lost the skills we used to have—not because we've gotten older, or we've lost our concentration, or because our minds are lazier, but because our minds have begun to think in a new way. We no longer sit by the fire and read Jane

Austen, because we are instead standing in line or riding on a bus, scrolling through a blog.

If you are a person who was already an adult when computers and smart phones arrived into your daily life, you may struggle with learning this new way of thinking. The older you are, the harder it may be for you. Some older people have decided to not go this route, and thus they are now left out of the wider conversation that is going on in the world—they are unable to access the information.

Conversely, if you are a person who grew up with computers and smart phones—if you can't remember a time these didn't exist, your mind may only know how to think this in the new way. If you've only known devices, you may find it hard to read a book, or to do research by hand. Even the idea of finding a location or trying to meet friend without your device may seem difficult. You may not know that it is easy to find your way simply by sensing, or that you can meet a friend through synchronicity—you have no frame of reference for working in this way.

Old ways, new ways. Neither is better or worse. They are just different styles of experiencing reality. However, they do reflect an evolution in human consciousness.

As a few more examples: decades ago, when I worked in advertising in Seattle, the ubiquitous "buckies" delivered documents throughout downtown via bicycle. Now of course, there is no need to hand carry information. Business is done by email or text. Decades ago we went to restaurants to eat, but now we order food from our phones and have a delivery person bring it over a few minutes later. Decades ago we called each other on land lines, and if we wanted privacy we used a phone with a very long extension cord. Later on, we graduated to a "cordless" phone, then a cell phone, now we have smart watches and A.I. in our home.

All of this has happened in mere decades—not even the cycle of a full generation.

We invented technology. Now technology is inventing us.

It can be scary to think of machines running our lives, or lack of privacy, or "big brother." Those are valid concerns. But human evolution due to the internet is not bad, or good. It just is. It's just the way humans are evolving right now. We can't stop shifting, we can't stop changing, we can't stop evolving. Everything changes, and this includes us.

However, when we do become aware of how our mind has changed—how the way we think has changed very quickly, over the last several decades—we can also understand that there are ways to work with this new mind, that are easy, meaningful and useful to us.

We can also understand what intelligent technology has been trying to make clear for a long time: our mind is actually "our" mind. Not just your mind, or my mind, but a new understanding of mind that is collective.

Our mind is collective mind.

Collective mind is collective soul.

Collective soul is the Universe/God/Divine/One/All.

You and I—personal Universes of consciousness that are entirely intertwined, connected and one with Universals consciousness—this is what we are learning now, as humans.

What we have begun to learn, as part of the internet revolution, is our own Oneness.

This is where we are evolving to.

In fact, many of us are already there.

Collective soul

One of the ways we know that we are experiencing collective soul, is that we have the same experiences when we journey. This is true when we journey without trying to, such as when we slip into a daydream, or when we dream at night. It's also true when we intentionally journey—when we go into a meditative state and intentionally try to connect with the Universe for guidance and help.

We know we are experiencing collective soul when we go to the same places beyond the veil, and we have the same types of experiences, and we utilize the same Universal language or symbolism to receive and process this information.

Now, I'm not talking about what happens in traditional meditation. Traditional meditation practices are also intentional journeys, and these journeys also take us to common collective portals. Volumes have been written about ancient spiritual traditions and the specific layers or levels of consciousness that can be reached in these journeys.

This type of journeying has been around for thousands of years, and there is great benefit to these practices.

However, what I am interested in is what the modern mind is doing—the mind that is starting to think a new way, as it begins to work with technology as a bridge to telepathy and collective soul experience.

Again, I believe ancient traditions have incredible value. If you enjoy them, use them. But I also believe that because we are modern people, it can be very useful to utilize modern practices that are more reflective of how our minds are working and evolving.

There is another difference as well. In many ancient practices, the goal of meditation was to seek bliss, nirvana, a state of altered consciousness where we became enlightened. However, in the journeying that I focus on, we are not initially seeking this kind of spiritual state. Nirvana is not our goal.

Instead, in the practice of intentional journeying in the etheric realms, we enter into Divine space, in order that we may be healed and guided by the Universe.

We enter in for Divine guidance.

We enter in for intuitive information.

We enter in to foreknow.

We enter in for direct knowing.

Of course, we also enter in to understand Oneness, but this is not really our goal, because Oneness happens every time we enter in. Every time we enter in we are enlightened—we do not need to achieve a "higher" state, because we are already experiencing complete Oneness, because that is who we are.

We already understand Oneness, and it's great to feel and sense that.

What we are learning now, is how to connect to the infinite wisdom of collective soul, to expand our own lives and the experience of the collective. We are beginning to learn to expand ourselves.

Part Two

Portals

Lesson 3

Common Portals

I understand that when we are discussing the mystic path, the language can get a little surreal. What is Oneness? Beingness? Collective consciousness? The Universe? All of these are big ideas, and it can be helpful to take a step back and just notice what are experiences are.

So if looking big is too hard, we can look small.

Because, of course, what is in the macro is in the micro.

The answers are there just the same.

For example, you can talk about collective soul all you want, and it will be a big blur to a lot of people—the terms are just too out there. But, if you ask people to look at a flower, to meditate on a flower and to connect with a flower—just a tiny flower!—you can see that they instinctively and naturally go into a place where they experience collective soul—Oneness with all the Universe—and they experience the healing and direct knowing that arrives from being in this state.

It can always be brought down to this level—by focusing on the small and the particular, we can also know the vast and ineffable.

Entering the realms

When we enter into Divine space intentionally, we usually find ourselves in common spaces. By this, I mean when we enter in, we usually enter in via the same doorways, and find ourselves in the same "welcoming areas" that are our entry points or gateways into the etheric realms.

We enter common portals.

This is something to keep in mind, as you do this work.

Knowing where you are starting—knowing how to find the doorway to your journey creates a wonderfully simple bridge for the mind. Knowing what gateway to use can a save you a lot of time and effort in this practice.

If you are familiar with shamanism, you already know that in order to enter the lower world, a common shared portal is to enter in at the root of a tree. If you've studied Akashic Records, you know there is a building you will enter. If you're heading to talk to the guides, there is a specific space you will meet. And so on. These are some of the more common gateways or entry points—there are so very many that we can use!

I began to pay attention to portals myself, because as I have mentioned before, when I first started working in the etheric realm, I really didn't know how I got there. As fast as blinking, I just went there. I would find myself instantaneously with my guide, and I wouldn't have a way to orient myself. I'd just dropped down the rabbit hole, my guide would be there, and I would have the experience. Eventually, I'd come out of it. During those years of early awakening, I didn't know how to repeat my journey or have it on demand. I had to wait until it happened again—out of the blue, with no warning or reason.

It was very frustrating to be at the whim of the Universe in this way!

And so I began to pay attention as best I could, so that I might crack the code journeying. How did it begin? What conditions were present? What conditions were absent? How did trance begin? What did the body feel like? And so on.

After a while, I began to channel in writing, and that was so much easier! When I channeled, I had a clear point of entry into the other realms. I could just sit on the sofa, open my laptop, close my eyes and breathe and I would instantly go "there" to where the guides were. This was repeatable and consistent—I could count on entering in every time I did this process, day after day. I have been channeling now for nearly 20 years, and it is as consistent as it has always been.

So, for me that was one method that worked—channeling in writing. For me, the writing itself is a trance, and it is a trance that is easy for me. It was as if I were playing music that I heard in my head, except it was writing—spiritual teachings.

However, when I was journeying in my mind's eye only, without the anchoring of writing and language, it took me longer to understand the process. It was a visual experience, seen in the mind's eye, and it required a different kind of paying attention. As I adjusted to the hazy view of third-eye seeing, and as my visioning began to become clearer and I began to be able to control the speed at which the information came in, I began to see familiar and consistent markers and signposts along the way.

I started to realize the body was part of this trance entrainment too—I was having a physical reaction every time I entered in: I might shake, or shudder, or sway. There would be some kind of physical shift in my earth body. I might feel different: I might notice the air got breezier, or I got colder. I started to recognize these physical changes with the moment I shifted dimensions, or rather more specifically, the moment before I transitioned. I have used that word "transitioned" before, as for those of you who've been in labor and had a baby, you know that the moment before it's time to push the baby, there is a moment of transition that is quite uncomfortable and has a distinct sensation of change. This is similar to how it feels right before you "enter in." The body has a physical reaction. It's not really unpleasant, it's just a feeling that something is changing—because it is.

Recall back to the "sonic boom" I experienced earlier, the exploding head syndrome that signified I was coming in or out of astral projection. We are Divine souls, but we are in physical bodies. So when we move through dimensions, we can expect some reactions in our physical container.

I have never found anyone to have a physically harmful experience exploring the astral realms. In fact, my belief is that exploring the etheric realms is very beneficial to the human form. Whenever we immerse ourselves in the Divine realms, we are filled with light at both the spiritual and physical levels.

After I started to notice that there would be a subtle physical response at the transition point between realms, I also started to notice where I was landing. I soon saw that the guides were taking me to the same places—the same portals—every time I entered in.

For definition, we might call a portal *a place between places*. A gateway, an entrance between the earthly and the Divine world.

At first, I thought these portals were unique to me—that the guides took me there, and that these were personal portals that no one else went to. What I found later, after teaching these techniques to so many people and sharing what we experienced, is that portals are not personal or unique.

We go to common portals that we experience as a soul collective.

I found, and still find, this to be tremendously exciting!

We go to the same places—we use the same bridges or entry points, because we are not separate, unique souls. We are collective soul. We use the same entry points, because we are One.

In shamanic tradition, there is a history of using portals as ways of beginning a journey. As mentioned earlier, some shamanic traditions use the portal of entering in through a root at the base of the tree of life. When you enter in this way, you find yourself in the lower world—the world of ancient times and plant and animal beings.

This is one way to get to this realm, and in fact it is one of my favorites. Yet, the tree root is the entry point—it is the portal that takes us there, and many, many people know how to use this portal. It is a common experience, a common portal.

That is exactly what we are seeking in this work—the common portals or places we go to as collective souls, to receive Divine information.

Common portals

So, what are some of the common portals?

Here are some that I have consistently noticed that I enter in to the realms—I have experienced them many times, and I have found that the people I have worked with also experience these portals.

You might think that our personal backgrounds might change the portals we experience, but this doesn't seem to be the case. What I have found is that regardless of background, age, gender, nationality—all the various ways we think we're different or separate—it doesn't seem to matter. These are common portals, experienced by the soul collective as common soul destinations. Here are some that I find the most common:

- The stone bench
- The still lake (or pond)
- The hut in the forest
- The Viewing Vista
- The tree of life
- The cave or cavern
- The white building
- The library
- The book
- The Viewing Room

- The river
- The blue planet
- The conference room
- The Universe

These sound like places we visit in fairy tales, don't they? As a child who grew up reading fairy tales and myths as the staples of my young literary experience, I am well aware that these portals we collectively explore are archetypal—they are memories held deep within the collective soul, not just for generations, but for generations of humans spanning thousands of years. They relate to our shared history as natural people—ancient people of the forests, of the meadows, of the caves. And yet, there is something more here—because we also find ourselves in buildings and libraries, and obviously these come from a later time in our collective history. And then later still, we find ourselves on planets, and in the Universe itself, and so either this is part of an even later or even earlier part of our history—when we were starseeds, new to the planet.

In any case, these portals—these common places we gather when we begin to journey—are held in soul memory by all of us. I would expect also, as we evolve as human, we will begin to visit other planets. We hold in soul memory what we've known or experienced since we arrived on this planet, whether as starseed or as part of human evolution. As we know more, our collective consciousness will expand, and we will have different portals that we commonly visit.

Now, the list above is not an exclusive list.

We also go to other places, all the time.

These are just the portals I most commonly see in my personal practice and when I am teaching others—these are what show up over and over again. I see or hear others reporting on these portals enough to realize there is a commonality—we are experiencing the same places and spaces, as a collective, over and over again.

I find it exceptionally interesting that people from all kinds of backgrounds go to these same portals—and this happens intentionally or not, with guidance or not, in a group or not, being aware of the portals or not. I find this phenomenon in the students I teach directly—they share their experiences with me, and it is always shocking to discover how similar their experiences can be—whether I am walking them through the meditation or they are doing it on their own.

Of course, where we visited in the past is likely different than where we visit now. And where we visit will change as we evolve. Basically, we are able to visit what we can understand—what we have evolved from that is contained in the collective mind, and what we can imagine now, that is moving into our sphere of evolution.

When we go into etheric space, we are able to see the future, and thus, we can also see future technologies, even things we can't imagine yet. But sometimes when we see future technologies we don't understand how they work, or what they do, and sometimes they are so outside of what we can imagine that we cannot see them. Think of the story of the Native Americans not being able to see the ships of Christopher Columbus as they sailed into the bay, because the idea of "ship" was not yet in the collective consciousness in that part of the world.

We often see things from the future, but because we do not have a frame of reference yet, we may not know what they are.

Traveling with guides

We will explore each of these portals in a moment. However, before we begin journeying, it's very important to establish the one rule that this work requires. Some of you know this rule already, but many of you don't.

It's the only rule I have, and this rule is paramount: in order to travel safely in the etheric realms, you must always have a guide with you.

There isn't an exception to this rule.

There isn't a grey area.

I myself am a person who doesn't like to follow rules, so this is a strong statement for me to make! However, after all of the experiences I've had both personally and in working with others, I believe it is paramount to safe, successful journeying.

Thus, I will say it again: *in order to travel safely in the etheric realms, you must always have a guide with you.*

You notice this is specific: you must have a *guide* with you. This is not the same as surrounding yourself in a bubble of light, or wearing a protective talisman, or saying a certain prayer, or smudging the room before you work, or repeating a mantra, or any of the other things we might do to protect ourselves.

This is about bringing in an actual guide—an advanced etheric being—to accompany you with you on your journey.

This guide—this being from multidimensional realms—is incredibly more elevated than you or me. Their vibrational level is higher—much higher than any human, departed or alive, can ever achieve, even those humans who are spectacularly evolved. Because of this, your guide will act as your wayshower, and also as your protector.

Your guide will hold the vibrational level at a high level—a level you cannot achieve by yourself—so that you can travel in light. If you try to travel by yourself, you will most certainly come across beings and entities and energies that are darker or draining forces. It is very difficult to energetically hold your own vibrational level when you are journeying, and when you are meeting beings and energies at different levels.

Your guide holds the vibration for you.

It is crucial that you have this protection, when you are journeying.

Connecting with guides

If you already know how to connect with your guide in the way I teach it (you can learn how in my book, *The Intuitive Path*), and are successfully able to call in your guide both on the fly and in deep meditation, connect with your guide now.

If you haven't done this style of guide work before, or you are familiar with guides but not with the style of work I do, no worries. You'll learn how in the next meditation. It isn't difficult, but it will open up the field so that you can find your way to your guide again and again.

Remember, we are part of collective soul. As you read this book, you are connecting with the other souls who are also reading this book, in whatever form it is in now or in the future.

What we practice right now—each of us, one at a time—is something that builds as an energy field. One person does this practice one day, another person does it the next day, someone else a week later, someone else 10 years later, someone else 100 years later.

Each time we practice, we add to the energy field that is this practice. As pioneer souls working in the energy field of collective soul, we are paving the way for more souls to do this work in the future. Again, every time you or I or others do this work, we connect into that energetic field of all souls doing this work, beyond all space, time and dimension.

This is very exciting!

Meditation: Calling in Your Guide

Each of us has many guides who show up to help us with different aspects of our lives, both as earth beings and infinite souls. Some other names for guides might be: spirit guides, angels, angelic realm, spirit master, ascended master. A guide is never a departed; guides have a vibration that is higher and more elevated than a departed, even if the departed is an advanced soul.

The name of your guide does not matter. You may or may not receive a name, and the name isn't important at all. The presence is all that matters.

During this meditation, you will be calling in a guide you can count on to help you any time you are journeying the etheric realms. Simply follow the instructions here, and you will meet a guide who will accompany you whenever you journey.

1. Find a quiet place where you can relax, and where you won't be interrupted. Sit in a way that's comfortable to you.

2. Close your eyes, and breathe in through the nose, and out through the mouth for at least three cycles. You will begin to feel a little floaty and woozy. Allow yourself to slip into this state. You will feel as if you are drifting.

3. Continue breathing in through the nose and out through the mouth in a natural way. Don't force it or pay attention to it too much. At a certain point, you will find you are not breathing in a particular way, and this is fine.

4. Now, begin to pay attention to the air in the room. The air is not nothing, it is filled with many souls, vibrations and other energies. Start to pay attention to the feeling of the breeze on your skin—your face, your hands, your arms. You will notice that it is slightly cooler, and you may feel a breeze where you didn't notice anything before.

5. Begin to pay attention to the vibration in the air in the room, such as noticing density of energies clustered in the room, on the ceiling, in a corner or elsewhere. Begin to pay attention to the vibration around your shoulders, to the sides, in front of you, and in back. When you find a density that feels different, just sit with that density. This is the energy of a guide. Feel into this energy and the characteristics of this presence, the same way you might identify the energy of a person who has come to stand beside you in a dark room—you can't see them, but you can sense then.

6. Now, shift your attention from the room, and bring your attention into your mind's eye—you might know this as your third eye, or you might just think of this as the place

where you "imagine" things in your head. Begin to sense or imagine what this guide looks like, with your thoughts or your imagination or your clairvoyance—the terms are not important. Sense who is there.

7. At this point, you will have the ability to discern some simple things about your guide: is this presence short or tall? Male, female or neutral? Wearing something specific, or wearing something general? Just notice. This will not be hard. The ideas will jump into your mind. Trust that your imagination is valid and is correct, and that there is no difference between imagination and clairvoyance. It is all third-eye seeing.

8. By this time, you will be able to sense your guide in the room, and sense your guide in your mind's eye. Connect with your guide, so there is a kind of telepathy between you.

9. At this point, your guide is with you and you are ready to begin your journey.

10. If you know how to journey, you can begin now. If you don't know how to journey yet, just stop for now. Bring yourself back to this reality by counting from 1 to 10, and relax.

11. When you are ready, continue reading. You will journey soon.

Lesson 4

Exploring the Portals

You can quickly become familiar with the common portals we visit as collective soul. When you are journeying, the faster you can identify where you are, the more quickly you can understand the bigger meaning of the guidance you are receiving.

For example, if you are journeying and find yourself in the *open meadow*, you will know that is neutral ground. There is nothing you need to pay attention to more than anything else. You'll just notice what happens as it happens. It is a safe, neutral space—a great place for beginning a journey.

However, if you find yourself in a *cavern*, this is a portal that is often associated with past life regression. The cavern is also used as gathering place for students and acolytes to be taught by guides. So, if you find yourself in a cavern, you might expect that you will go on a past life regression, or you may be taught an esoteric skill in a group of student souls. Knowing what to expect helps your orient yourself to what may happen.

Or, if you find yourself in the *river*, you will know that is a distinctive portal that most often refers to the flow of birth to death—the river of life, or in some text, the River Bardo. Again, knowing what to expect helps you orient yourself to what may happen.

Let's take a brief view of the portals now. As you read the description for each portal now, take a moment and see if it feels familiar to you. Sense if you've been there before. Chances are, you're going to be familiar with most, if not all, of these portals.

You'll want to do this sensing in a relaxed, easy way. We'll be exploring the portals more deeply later on, so you don't need to take a lot of time with this. As you read about the portals, just notice where there's resonance. You might ask yourself, "Have I been here?" or "Is this place familiar to me?" You might wonder, "Have I visited this place in a dream? A memory? A past life?" You will be familiar with many of these portals, and others you might not have visited yet. Again, we'll visit them all in depth later. For now, read along, open your mind and let the information float through.

The open meadow

This is the most common, neutral portal. You simply find yourself in an open space that I and many others describe as an open meadow. There's not a lot to describe here. The open meadow doesn't have specific flowers or grasses. It's a somewhat generic field. The sky is big—it's cloudless and easy. The sun is up, but it's not hot. In the distance, I can see the edges of a forest, but the forest is not descriptive or important. It's just there. To the left, I often see a white building, but not always. The meadow just is. It is a safe place to land, and the most common and fastest way I meet my guides. I show up in the meadow, and they are there waiting for me, or they start to walk forward from the left or front to where I am. You can trust you are in a safe, neutral place where it is easy to commune with your guides and angels, if you find yourself in the meadow. In general, the meadow is a place of infinite possibility. Anything could happen—you might join your guide and have information or guidance revealed, or you might be taken on a journey from the meadow to a new place. It is a place of positivity and safety.

The stone bench

The stone bench is a place where you will receive direct, personal guidance from your guide or guides. This is the place where the Universal *tête-à-tête* will happen—you will find yourself approaching a bench where a guide will be sitting and waiting for you, or you and your guide will walk together to a bench and you will sit together and talk. This is the place of Divine counsel, a place to reveal what is in your heart, a place to receive information that will help you move forward. Of course, the guide already knows what is in your heart, but there is something about begin able to say your heart's truth, that is so very healing for all of us. Personal counsel is what happens when you visit the stone bench. This is a place of compassion and kindness, where you will feel supported.

The still lake (pond)

The still lake or pond is a mirroring portal. The archetypes of collective soul you might experience here might remind you of Greek gods looking into ponds, or Arthur sending his sword to the lake. The lake is watery, feminine, receptive and calm. It is a place to reflect upon your journey, and to receive reflections. For example, your guide may direct you to look into the water, and see yourself or something else reflected back to you. Your guide may also direct you to give the water something. Finally, the lake is always a sign of healing and baptism. You may be asked to submerge yourself, to heal, cleanse, release or be baptized. As a less common version of the lake/pond, you may also experience a waterfall. This is a more active version of this same portal.

The hut in the forest

The hut in the forest is a portal that exists in both space and time. A visit there may often reveal your life's work and life's purpose, although this is not always the case. The hut in the forest may also be an entry point into a past life. Usually, you will come upon the hut (again, it's archetypal. Think Hansel and Gretel, or any fairy tale you've read where the main character comes across a small dwelling and then goes inside.). Inside the hut, you will be met by a guide. What is interesting about the hut, is that it always contains objects: a fire may be burning, there may be a table and chairs, a bed for resting, cups and plates and other simple items. You may be invited to eat a simple repast with your guide. It is common, though not what always happens, to notice a similarity in the work taking place in the hut, to what your life's work is now. For example, you may notice a pen and paper on a rough table, and this may provide a clue to you to continue your writing work in this lifetime. The hut is both a portal in space and a portal in time. It is a safe place, a place of simple comfort, protection and pause, and you may be asked or allowed to rest there for a while, especially if you are in need of rest.

The Viewing Vista

The Viewing Vista is a magical and visionary portal, and may take you on a longer and more intensive journey beyond the vista itself—in fact, this is what usually happens. If you are about to enter the portal that is The Viewing Vista, you will be met by a guide, and the guide will accompany you up a mountain path, until you reach an overlook or view point. As you look down at the scene or valley below, you may see clouds or weather covering your view. In a while, the clouds or weather will open and you may see a town or village below, or you may see something else. Your guide will then take you on a journey in which you can fly down into the valley—you might fly there in an astral body, or you might fly there as a point of consciousness—and then you can explore what you are meant to see there. For example, you might explore the buildings or other areas of the town, as part of your journey. You might enter a building, then a room, and then find someone or something there that is meaningful to you.

What is key about The Viewing Vista, is that you may go on the journey to the vista point, or you may travel further into what is below in the valley. You will receive the information fully, either way. Finally, The Viewing Vista will often take you into future lives—there is a magical, ancient-yet-new aspect of this portal, and you will often see things you have never seen or imagined before, as they are in the future of this particular lifetime.

The white building

The white building is well-recognized as a manifestation of the Akashic Records, which many people consider to be the energetic holding place for the history of human consciousness—every event, action, memory, intention and emotion are recorded and stored in the Akashic Records. My experience is that the Akashic Records is not limited to human consciousness—it is really just another name for the One Soul that is the Universe. Of course everything is there, because it is everything. In another way of looking at it, the Akashic Records isn't really a portal; it is what exists in every moment, as our infinite Nowness as souls. In another way of thinking of it, since humans work so well in symbolism and metaphor and archetype as their soul language, it is very useful to have a white building we can enter, to help us ground in our experience better. Many people feel the white building has a Greek or Roman feeling, while others will have a different reference point. In any case, the white building is usually entered via the meadow, and inside there are many rooms and areas to explore, including but not limited to The Book of Knowledge, the library, The Viewing Room and more.

The Book of Knowledge

The Book of Knowledge is another portal in The Akashic Records, which once again, is the Universe. The Akashic Records, the library, the book and The Viewing Room are not separate or different from any of the other portals. There is really only one portal, which is moving into consciousness. However, for purposes of ease of use, the book is a very fun, magical and simple tool. Basically, you will be guided to look at a book in The Akashic Records. This book is your personal book, it is the record of you as a soul. All your lifetimes are in the book—all your thoughts, ideas, emotions, intentions, actions, everything. When you look at the book, you will be directed to a particular page that contains information that is important for you to have now. It may show you a memory of the past. It may show you something happening now. It may show you the near future. Most books will have writing and imagery, but you may not be actually able to read or see these—it is more an impression of the meaning that is clear to you. Sometimes, you will find yourself entering into the writing or the imagery, and going on the journey that awaits you there. You can simply jump into or enter into the image, or the text, and go into that dimension to explore.

The library

The library lies within the Akashic Records building. You will usually experience it as a room with long tables and chairs to sit at to study, and walls and walls of books, covered floor to ceiling. Unlike an old library, which may be dark or dusty, the library is pristine—the books may be old but they are immaculate, as if they are cleansed with Light.

The books contain all the knowledge of the world—and I believe, of the Universe. You can look at all the books that you as a soul are ready to see. Different souls can look at different books. The library is infinite and eternal.

Once again, the library is really the Universe, which is Oneness, which is everything. We don't need to use the library as a portal to gather this information—we already know it, because we are also it. However, the human mind finds it easier to work in archetype and metaphor, and so the library is a very useful tool to sort as we meditate and gather information. You can go to any section of the library that is available (your guide will let you know, or you will be unable to access sections that are not available) and you can pull out any book and read whatever information you want to know. Usually the information is received as telepathy or knowing—you do not read in the same way you are reading now. It is an instantaneous absorption of the information.

The Viewing Room

The Viewing Room is a room or area in The Akashic Records, where it is very easy to see past, present and future lifetimes. I experience The Viewing Room as room with a gigantic, floor-to-ceiling window, and beyond that window there is a scene from my life—from memory or from past or future lives. When I watch through The Viewing Window, a guide stands to my side and may provide commentary. I can watch what is happening, like a live movie or play is being performed in front of me. Sometimes I am a participant in the memory or foreknowing, sometimes not.

The Viewing Room is most commonly used as a time portal—it allows you to be the observer and also the participant, at whatever level you desire or are guided to work in. For example, if the guide takes you to The Viewing Room, and you are currently work on your relationship with your mother, your guide may show you a series of memories that you may have forgotten, which provide you with new information about your relationship to your mother. This is just one example.

You may see The Viewing Room as an overview when the guides want you to view situations as soul, or you may enter The Viewing Room and become a part of the experience, if the guides want you to have a more emotional experience. One of the most interesting things about The Viewing Room is its ability to show you so many memories you may not actively remember. This is invaluable when you are looking into the hows and whys of your lifetime.

The Tree of Life

The tree of life has a grand tradition in both Kabbalah and shamanic journeying. In the journeying we do in spiritual intuition, it is most often used as a portal. Its second use is as a wisdom being—a conscious entity that is a representation of the Universe itself. The tree of life is usually a massive maple or oak or other deciduous tree. However, I have worked with portals where the tree of life was a palm tree on the banks of the Nile River, or a tiny Christmas tree growing on a tree farm in Oregon, and so many other variations. The tree species itself will usually have some significance to you. The tree of life will most often serve as a portal—as an entry point into an etheric realm. If you enter deep in the roots, you will usually go into the lower world, which we will discuss further—in general, this is the realm of the plants and animals. If you enter into a knot-hole or other entry point further up, you may come across other beings such as the elemental world of fairies and elves. If you enter via the leaves you may find yourself working with light and the light beings of Nature. And, of course, there are other variations. As a wisdom being, you may ask the tree of life any question, the same as you would a guide. It is a guide. Finally, you may work with the tree of life as an imaginal being, in your mind's eye, or as a physical being—a real tree you know and visit in nature. We will discuss this more soon.

The cave or cavern

The cave is often an invitation to meditate very deeply, while the cavern is most often a portal into past lives. You may experience several versions of this portal, depending on what your past lives have been. For example, if you've had a lot of past lives in a Buddhist or Hindu tradition, you may find yourself in a small meditation cave, similar to what a monk or hermit in those times might inhabit. This is a personal cave—a guide will be with you, but otherwise you will be in a remote area, and you will be invited to go deeply into your connection with the Universe—perhaps more deeply than you've ever been before. If you find yourself instead in a gigantic cavern, you will commonly see many other guides—not just yours—and also may other souls. The cavern is a common gathering spots for many souls together, especially as a portal for group teaching.

The river

The river is an intense portal, as it symbolizes the passing of your life from birth to death. More specifically, it shows the Flow of your life, as it is happening now and in the near future, as you move through time. The river is infinite; it contains all of your lifetimes, one after another, for infinity.

Sometimes, the river is experienced as the River Bardo, which in Tibetan Buddhism refers to the state of the soul between death and rebirth. However, this is more uncommon. Usually, people who enter the river portal are only able to see the current stream or flow they are actively living in now. It becomes a living metaphor for what is going on Now.

The river is not consistent—time and place and emotion will change. Sometimes you will be on a wide section of the Nile River, for example; another time on a narrow forest stream in Europe, and so on. As with all of these portals, everything is symbolic. What you are floating on, who or what is on the banks, what the weather is like, if the water is smooth or turbulent—every single detail provides metaphoric or symbolic or archetypal information on your current relationship to Flow in your life.

The blue planet

The blue planet is a strange portal that is often a place souls go to for group gatherings. For example, if I am leading a group meditation, I am often directed by the guides to take the group into space, and then to land down on the blue planet. Everything on the planet is blue. I believe that the blue color relates to the vibrational level that is required to do this kind of work; when we align with the color, we align with the frequency. The blue planet is a portal where groups of students work on a soul level with their guides. There are certainly other planets, such as the green planet, the indigo planet, the pink planet, the white planet—working our way up from the heart chakra with the colors associated with those chakras, but I have not visited those with frequency; the blue planet is where I am most often directed to go.

The conference room

The conference room is another small portal in space. It is used for soul to soul communication with a guide or guides present. It is often not even a conference—it may simply present as a table with chairs, or sometimes nothing at all—just you, your guide or guides, and the other soul or souls you are working with. This is also a very common portal for working with ancestral lineages.

The Universe

The Universe does not communicate in human language; it is not symbolic, metaphoric or archetypal. We just perceive it this way, because this is the soul language we currently understand as humans. It is a way we can make sense of the Universe. But sometimes, we can let go of this symbolic and emotional soul language, and experience the Universe as it really is—as pure consciousness. This happens when we are in very expanded states, and we are able to let go of the soul language and simple experience the Universe in its vast energetic state. By vast state, I mean both the particulate energy state of everything and the infinite energy state of everything, both of which are the same thing.

The big, the small, the particulate, the vast, the past, the future, the you, the we. All One, all the time. We can dissolve into this, and we do this all the time. We just dissolve, and become one with everything. This experience of the Universe is not so much portal, as an experience of letting go of all soul language, all belief, all illusion, all veil, and simply experience ourselves as Oneness.

As you reviewed each of the portals that we commonly visit, you probably had a sense of familiarity or déjà vu, a sense of "oh, I've been there." This is because of course you have, many times in this lifetime and in your many past lifetimes. You go to these portals in the liminal states of dreams, trance and so on. But you can also choose to go to these portals, Intentionally and specifically, as part of your soul practice.

Let's try this now so you can see what it feels like.

Meditation: The Open Meadow

For this journey, we'll go to the open meadow.

The open meadow is considered a neutral portal—it's a dimension where things begin. Because of this, it is normal for there not to be a lot of action. For example, if you are met by a guide in the open meadow and taken on a journey, great. But if most of your experience in the open meadow is simply noticing your environment that is just fine too.

The open meadow is a portal where it is very easy for the guides and other beings to meet us and to communicate with us, and also very easy for us to meet and communicate with them. In essence, it is a vibrational plane. Whenever you go up the two steps to the open meadow, you are aligning your vibration with the guides, and vice versus.

Aligning vibration is the key to successful journeying. However, alignment is not hard. There is nothing particular to pay attention to. You simply decide to raise your vibration—and the moment this is your intention, this becomes your reality.

Remember you are always a soul, and your soul knows how to travel and journey, and does so all the time. You do not need to teach it. You simply need to allow it. Your soul knows the way.

As a caveat, remember to call in your guide for every journey you take. This is already built into the instructions for this meditation.

1. Find a quiet place where you can relax, and sit in a way that's comfortable to you.

2. Close your eyes, and breathe in through the nose, and out through the mouth for at least three cycles.

3. Now, imagine that there is a step that you will step up onto; we will call this step level one, the vibration of peace and tranquility. Notice what this step looks like, what it is made of. Step up onto this level.

4. Imagine there is a second step; we will call this step level two, the vibration of love and light. Notice what this step looks like, what it is made of. Step up onto this level.

5. As you look around from where you are on the second step, you can see that there is another space opening up and revealing itself to you. This is the open meadow. This open space may have a field of grasses or wildflowers, or something else. Notice what kind of vegetation you see. Pay attention to anything that appears different or surprises you. Is there a particular kind of grass or flower? Are there insects or small animals? What else?

6. Notice also that your guide is with you. You do not need to interact with your guide, just notice that he or she is there. If your guide is not visible to you yet, remember to call him or her in. Sometimes you will have a familiar guide that you know, sometimes you will have a more generic guide for journeying. It's okay either way.

7. As you look further into your surroundings, you may notice that the sky is open, sunny or clouded. What is the sky like?

8. As you look further, you may notice a forest in the far distance; this may have evergreen trees, or another kind of tree. Notice what kind of trees, or what the forest feels like to you. What do you notice?

9. As you look further, to the far left, you may notice a white building or something else. We are not going there in this journey, but just bring it into your awareness. Can you see or sense it?

10. Finally, stand in the open field, and allow yourself to expand into the entire environment. Simply pay attention to everything, all at once. If something starts to happen, go with that.

11. Recall that the open field is a place of neutral beginnings, and often something will begin to lead you into another aspect of your journey. For example, a guide may want you to travel with him or her, a spirit animal may appear, an insect may show up, a flower may catch your attention, and so on. Just notice anything that calls to you, and follow it.

12. If you have a question you would like guidance on, now is the time to ask for information that will be helpful to you. You might say "tell me about this" or "what is my best understanding about this?"

13. Receive whatever information, sense, memory, vision or knowing that arrives to you.

14. When you are ready, say goodbye to your guide, head out of the open meadow, back down onto step two, back down onto step one, and back into your body. Count yourself back to this reality by counting back from 10 to 1. Open your eyes.

15. As soon as you are able, journal on what you saw or experienced in the open meadow.

Part Three

Soul Language

Lesson 5

Soul Language

As soul travelers in the Universe, we communicate with soul languages. As humans, our soul language includes language, symbolism, metaphor, archetype, action, emotion and energy. Obviously, there are many soul travelers in the Universe who are not human, who may have different, lower or higher methods of communication, but as humans, we are only able to speak and understand in the way that we can.

In general, the soul language we as humans can use at any given time, relates to our vibrational state. The higher the state we can go to, the more we can understand. However, this does not mean we need to go into the highest vibrational state, in order to communicate with the Universe! In fact, we can go very, very slightly out of our earth reality, and have great success in receiving Divine guidance.

By this, I mean we can enter into a vibrational state that is slightly higher than our everyday state—we might have our eyes closed, we might do some deep breaths—but we're not going deep. We're just in the lightest trance.

This is the optimal state to be in, to do this kind of soul journeying.

You will know you are in this state, when if you tried to get up, you might have to reorient yourselves to where you were, or if the phone rang you might have to reorient yourself to answer it, but mostly you come out of this light meditative state very easily.

You're in, you're out.

You're in, you're out.

It's easy to go back and forth.

So, in this light trance state, we find the balance. If we hover too close to the earth plane, we become too grounded to access etheric information. If we lift off too far into the etheric realm, we lose our ability to receive with our earth mind.

Why is this important? Primarily, because the trance state you enter will determine the kind of information you receive from the Universe.

When we communicate with the Universe in soul language, we find there are several ways we, as humans, can receive understanding:

- Language
- Symbolism
- Metaphor
- Archetype
- Motion
- Emotion
- Energy

Let's take a look at each of these briefly.

Language

Language is what we understand as words. Telepathy is language, channeling uses language, and direct knowing often arrives as a kind of language. Many people notice that language arrives in meditation in one ear or the other, as a voice in the mind that is not one's own voice, or as a telepathy from guides or spirits.

Symbolism, metaphor and archetype

Symbolism, metaphor and archetype are all "short cuts" or quick ways the Universe communicates ideas to us. For example, if we see an object in meditation that looks like an apple, this may be a symbolic or metaphoric apple. For example, an apple may relate to Adam and Eve, a teacher's apple, an apple a day for health, an Adam's Apple, and so on.

If a guide shows up in our meditation, this guide is likely archetypal: he or she has an archetypal identity that we understand and relate to as part of our collective soul. As a common example, we might see a Native American guide, who is archetypal for an ancient, tribal, earth-centric guide. If we see a guide in a monk outfit, we understand this is archetypal for a monastic, religious, ancient guide. If we see a guide who looks like Mother Mary, we understand this is archetype for the mother of Jesus, purity, and the Divine feminine.

Most symbols, metaphors and archetypes are instantly understood by us, because they are part of our collective soul understanding as humans, or part of our personal experience in this lifetime or other lifetimes. If we receive a symbol, metaphor or archetype we don't understand or haven't seen before, when we research it a bit we usually find that it is actually something familiar to us.

Motion

Motion is what happens when we see or vision things happening in meditation—when things start to move. Some people see motion immediately—they jump into visions that start moving and morphing. Other people see static images for a while, and then they begin to become aware of motion. Whenever you see something moving or changing in your meditation, follow along with what is happening. Seeing motion in meditation will become the norm for you after just a few practice sessions, if not the first time you try it.

Emotion

Emotion is just what it sounds like—a welling up of feeling that comes over you as you journey. Emotion is a good sign in meditation, and may bring you healing or release from a past situation or relationship; you will probably feel better afterwards. If you do experience emotion that is sticky, uncomfortable or unpleasant, this is how the Universe shows you that a situation or relationship is not safe or healthy for you.

Energy

Energy is high vibrational soul language—it has no words, symbolism, metaphor, archetype. It may have motion and emotion, and for some people it has color or another way of seeing or sensing density. We can work with energy and in energy, but it is harder to interpret energy as we do the other soul languages. We are simply too far "out there" in vibration, to understand it as clear intuitive information. We would instead begin to work with it in energy healing, which is a complex topic for a future time.

Why vibration matters

Your ability to understand soul language is directly related to your vibrational level. Most people think higher vibration is better—but in this work, that isn't the case. Enter a very light trance state, and we have the ability to use language. But go too high into the etheric realms—go too deep into trance—and we start to lose our ability to use language. So, if you want to have telepathy with your guides, or hear or see words, or channel in voice or writing, the lightest trance is all you'll need.

The deeper we go into trance, i.e., the higher we go up in vibrational level, the more we lose our ability to use soul language. First, we lose the ability to understand language, then we lose the ability to use symbolism, metaphor, archetype and motion, then we lose the ability to receive emotion, and finally, we move to a vibrational state where we can only access energy.

I want to explain that there are no strict "levels" when this starts to happen. It is not as if you can take three breaths and be in the place where you can use language, while five breaths will make you lose that ability. This work is fluid. You have to experiment with your own unique vibrational style, and notice what you're experiencing.

And, it's also not that working in a high vibrational state is bad—it's not! Many traditional meditation practices choose to go to a high vibrational level and marinate in that energy, and this is a great practice. A lot of energetic healing happens there.

However, if your intention is to gather intuitive information or Divine guidance, you will need to take care that you do not allow your vibrational level to climb too high. The easy way to test it? If you can't see your guides, you've gone too high. If you can't see motion, you've gone too high. And so on. While you are in trance, you can keep checking what you can access, and if you are finding you are just in a floaty state where there is no information, you will want to bring yourself back to earth a bit.

This is not difficult to regulate. You can simply say "bring me back" or think "I need to come back to my earth self a little."

There aren't a lot of rules and regulations in this work. Once you've entered in and experienced receiving information, you'll know how to go to that dimensional level again. You'll simply be able to sense it. You'll be able to feel your way. You'll also be able to feel if you get too far out there, and you'll be able to adjust.

For me, after so many years of doing this work, the practice has become instantaneous. It's as the saying goes: once you know how to ride a bike, you don't forget. You can simply hop on the bike and ride it. For me, I no longer need to breathe in and out or close my eyes to "enter in," the way I did when I first started. Now, I can just "go there" at will. Once I am "in," I can simply adjust my levels, according to how I want to gather intuitive information. I don't need to try or even think about—I can just set my intention and this is what happens.

This is what will happen for you, too.

Maybe not the first time, but soon. After a little bit of practice, it will become second nature for you. You may find you have to revert to implementing more structure if you are over tired, over stressed, or haven't had enough sleep. In those cases, you might have to work a little harder to enter in. Curiously, you may find that in high stress or emergency situations, this ability to "go there" seems to ramp up, and in fact can be significantly accelerated.

The more we practice and experiment in this realm, the more familiar it becomes and the more easily we can navigate within it. What is especially nifty (and the main reason I am doing and teaching this work) is that the more we experience this realm, the more we all have the ability to experience these realms! As collective soul, we have collective experiences. As one soul expands, the more we all expand! Your own practice helps elevate the energy for everyone, and vice versus.

So, if you are struggling to "see" or "hear" as we move along in this practice, consider that you may be going too deep, instead of not deep enough. If you go only to the slightest edge of the state you might feel is "trance" that is fine—that is the right place! If you go further, you will find yourself in a different vibrational level, where language and symbolism won't be available to you.

You can still work in this realm, but it will be only energetic, and you may not remember what you receive.

As a final recap: Light trance is ideal for intuitive gathering. Deeper trance is ideal for healing. As we raise vibrational level, we first lose language, then we start to lose symbolism, metaphor and archetype, next we lose emotion and finally we even lose our ability to work in energy. If your goal is intuitive gathering, you'll have best results in a very light trance. You don't need to do lengthy, deep meditations to do this work of intuitive gathering—of soul travel—and nothing could be further from the truth. Light, quick, easy and relaxed brings the best results.

Part Four

Symbol,
Metaphor,
Archetype

Lesson 6

Gifts and Objects

Gifts and objects are ways the Universe communicates with us symbolically and metaphorically. Every time you journey, you will likely be presented with at least one gift or object that will contain the core essence of the message you are receiving.

The Universe uses these symbolic structures or energetic containers as short cuts, as a way of communicating meaning clearly and quickly.

There are two ways this can happen: if you receive a gift at the very start of a journey, just as you are heading into a portal, it is likely not very important—it is a generic or neutral gift that may be presented as energetic support, but have no significant meaning.

Its purpose is not to provide meaning—it's more of an energetic or vibrational boost.

However, if you are deeper into your journey, and have already gone into to a portal and met with a guide, and then the guide presents you with a gift, it will be quite meaningful and important. Again, the gift or object will contain the core essence of the message you are receiving.

Following, I've presented a list of some common gifts we often receive. Again, the Universe uses these gifts as short cuts—they are understood by collective soul, and because of this, they will be very easy for you to understand. These gifts and their meanings are part of collective consciousness, the same way collective portals are. They are embedded in our ancestral memory, our soul memory.

However, there are other gifts that arrive outside of this list. First, the list is not complete—it is culled from the common gifts that show up over and over in the journeying that I have been teaching for decades, based on the gifts received by thousands of students from all over the world.

It's a good list, and it shows what resonates with many people, but it is only a starting point.

This is because most of you will receive gifts that are not common—you will receive gifts that are personal to you—by this, I mean are personal to your history, your life events, your memories and your emotions—and the meaning of these gifts will also be personal and specific to you.

I know you're getting eager to know more; we'll discuss some examples of gifts in just a moment.

First (and this next part is a little esoteric but also important to our understanding) there's a little bit more about vibration, time, space and matter.

Vibration, time, space, matter

Vibrationally, objects show up in vibrational match to everything else in your journey. You sense the portal in your mind's eye and when it's at a certain vibration, you sense a guide in your mind's eye and he or she is at a matching vibration, you sense an object in your mind's eye, and that vibration matches, too.

In terms of **time**—objects show up in relational time to us—in a time frame we can understand. By this, I mean, if an object shows up, it will either be from the past, the present or the near future—these are all time frames we are familiar with. We will experience the object as now, but we will have a way of identifying what time it is from. Sometimes objects show up from the future that we may pre-recognize, such as a healing tool that doesn't exist yet, but we can tell it's for healing, or a communication tool that doesn't exist yet, but we can tell it's for communicating, as examples. However, in general, we won't receive an object that we don't understand—we will have some familiarity with what it is and does.

In terms of **space** and **matter**, both are very fluid in journeying. There is not much density in what we experience when we journey. This is very similar to how you experience space and matter in a sleeping dream, but in journeying you can track better and have more awareness.

For example, objects are often flying around or don't have a lot of gravity. A heavy table might be lightweight. Objects might show up in your journey, but they may fly away, disappear, come closer, go further, be weightless. Space and how we experience space relationship is always shifting. A tree may fly, for example, instead of being rooted into the ground. Matter is not dense— everything is a mirage or apparition. It's real, but it's not earth real.

We can move through space and matter very quickly, or instantly. For example, we may move through a wormhole or shimmering strand or ribbon of energy, and simply find ourselves in another space. Or another space may simply appear. So, space is very fluid in journeying.

There is a great deal to say about vibration, time, space and matter when journeying. However, I am not a quantum physicist. I am a soul traveler who has spent most of my life journeying, without thinking about string theory or God particles or other scientific notions. It is okay to approach this work as an artist, a dreamer, or an explorer. This is the work of the soul pioneer, the soul traveler, and it is enough to explore and continue to explore, and to allow the Universe to show you what you need.

List of common gifts and objects

Some of the most common are gifts that we understand as collective soul are:

- The cup or goblet
- The bowl
- The flower
- The apple or fruit
- The acorn or stone
- The fairy or pixie
- The box or chest
- The book
- The feather or pen
- The ball or orb
- The ring
- The sword
- The staff
- The cloak
- Other gifts

We'll cover these fully in a moment.

When gifts show up

When we are in the process of raising vibration as we enter into and begin a journey, it is very common to notice an object such as a cup or bowl or flower showing up. This happens during the process of entering in, before you find yourself in a portal.

In other words, these gifts show up at the start of your journey. And, if we aren't ready to pay attention, we might miss them altogether. So, it's important to look around and see if there is anything to notice as you enter in.

For example, when I close my eyes and breathe and begin the process of entering into a light trance, but right before I step into whatever portal I am visiting, I will often notice a cup or bowl swirling around in the air.

Objects received during this time frame aren't usually symbolic or metaphorical—they aren't usually meaningful. Instead, they simply provide energetic or vibrational support during the transition between earth and etheric realm.

The most common object that shows up at this time is a cup or bowl—it's usually just floating around in the air.

The meaning of this cup or bowl is not always significant, but I believe it is an infusion of vibrational sustenance. It is usually filled with some kind of elixir, which I am invited to drink. I simply notice the cup floating around, I notice it is filled with liquid, I drink it, and then continue on into the journey.

Simple, straightforward, and with a quality of neutrality.

There's no great "aha" for me when I notice a cup or bowl. Again, that quality of neutrality—the object feels helpful, but not symbolically important.

There is not much to do here—as you enter into your journey, simply take a moment to notice if you see something flying around or hanging in the air. If something is there, just interact with it. If it's a cup, drink from it. If it's a bowl, eat from it. If it's a pixie or fairy, say hello. If it's a flower, smell it, and so forth.

Gifts received from guides

The gifts and objects that are given to you by your guides show up later in your journey, and these are the ones to pay attention to. These are the gifts that will have deep significance and meaning, and will relate directly to the core message of your journey.

Why do guides use gifts?

Think of it this way: your guides want to provide you with an answer to your question—either an intentional question that you've asked at the start of your journey, or the question that is deep in your heart—and they want to do this in the fastest, clearest way possible.

They have to work quickly, because the human ability to stay in trance is not very developed—we cannot stay in light trance very long, before either our minds begin to wander and we come out of trance, or we go in very deep where we can no longer access language or symbolism. So, the guides know they have a limited—a few minutes to perhaps 30 minutes—time when we can actively gather intuitive information without losing our concentration or needing a break.

When I first teach a group of students, I am satisfied if I can keep the group in a state of intuitive gathering for 20 minutes before taking a break. When a group has been working together for a while, such as in the training I teach, the power of the group supports a much longer meditation. This is because we enhance each other's ability to stay in trance—this is similar to when we sing a collective "om" in a group— each member picks up when another takes a breath and in this way the om can continue a very long time. So too, when journeying in a group each member holds concentration when another falters, and so the group members continually support each other in maintaining the correct level of trance for intuitive gathering. Get a group of people who've meditated together for a long time, and you can stay in trance for a very long time.

However, intuitive gathering is a different kind of work than traditional meditation, and even the most seasoned intuitive gatherers—in a group or on their own—will begin to have gathering fatigue after a certain point.

So, be aware that it is okay to work quickly, and it is okay to not stay in trance too long. Especially if you're working by yourself, you may not be able to stay in trance that long. Thus, the guides will want to get the core information to you quickly—and the fastest way they can do this is by using symbolism and metaphor.

Why don't they just use language, you might wonder?

When we experience language with the guides, it is not very complex. You might get one word, such as "being" or "oneness," or you might receive a short phrase, such as "go to school" or "slow down" or "be kind." But complex ideas, such as "it's time for you to go back to school and get your master's" are more difficult for us to receive. An even deeper thought, such as "it's time for you to truly value your self-worth and follow your heart's true longing and your soul's destiny, and do something that allows you to break the pattern of your mother and grandmother and all women ancestors before you, and to go back to school and get your master's so that you can support all women and also yourself," takes a long time to communicate at the practical, emotional and spiritual level. So, as a short cut, your guides may instead show you a graduation cap, and as they place it onto your head you feel all the support of all the women in your family for generations—you feel your own heart swell with how this is your true longing. It is a lot to be communicated, and this is why a symbolic image can be a faster way to condense and deliver the information.

(Note: if you *are* a person who has been thinking of getting their master's degree, I would take the above information as a very direct sign to do so. The examples I write in the book are always brought to me from the Universe; I do not know who you are, but I know that this information is definitely meant for one or many of you reading this book or this information at some later time).

Common gifts and objects

Now, let's take a closer look at the gifts you are likely to receive from your guides, and what their common meaning is as understood by collective soul.

The cup or goblet

The cup or goblet provides us with a liquid or elixir to drink. This is a way of receiving sustenance from the Universe. Some of you may have the association of communion, or drinking from a Divine chalice. For others, it may be more similar to how a runner grabs an offered cup of water as he runs past a checkpoint in a race. It's just a supportive liquid. We are offered, we take it, we imbibe it. There is usually not much more to it than this; however, sometimes there is. Sometimes, when you drink from the cup or goblet, it will be a Divine experience—an etheric level of communion and healing. There is nothing to do differently— just drink from the cup if it is offered, and notice what happens.

The bowl

The bowl is like the cup but its sustenance is heartier. The bowl feeds you—not physically, but emotionally and spiritually. If you receive the bowl, eat from it. The Universe is giving you emotional and spiritual nourishment that you may not have known you needed. You may feel warmer, whole or grounded when you eat from the bowl, or you might feel nothing different. Just notice what happens.

The flower

The flower has a delicacy of spirit that helps raise vibration. Different flowers may show up for you, but in the most neutral, generic sense of flower you will most often see a delicate, petaled flower that is small and sweet. If you are familiar with Bach's floral remedies, this is a way to think about the flower—it is a consciousness that is revealed in a beautiful and gentle flower. If you receive a flower, you might hold it in your hand, tuck it in your pocket or in other ways take it with you on your journey. It is a symbol of tender, loving, high-vibrational support to you.

The apple or fruit

Most often, the apple or fruit relates to health and nourishment. It is an invitation to eat plant based, or to increase the amount of nutrition in your diet—especially to eat raw and plant foods. Sometimes, the apple will also be related to teaching or education, such as the apple we used to bring to a teacher, or the apple that was the fruit on the tree of knowledge. But more often, it is about nourishing yourself with clean, high-vibrational foods, especially fruits and vegetables.

The acorn or stone

Like the flower, the acorn or stone are meant to be taken with you on your journey. They are small, concentrated pieces of energy that you can tuck in your pocket or hold in your hand. The acorn, of course, is about possibilities—from the tiny acorn, a mighty oak grows. The stone is pure comfort—grounding, earthy, stable, securing. If you continually come across an acorn or stone in your journeying, you might consider carrying around an acorn or stone in your pocket in your real life, too. As above, so below.

The fairy or pixie

Tiny beings—fairies, pixies, leprechauns, sprites and so forth—often show up just as we enter the transition into our journey. They show up to support us, and to help us vibrationally ascend to the higher realms. If you're not familiar with the elemental world, you might think of fairies and pixies as small etheric helpers. Sometime, fairies and pixies help us raise our vibration, because they remind us of fun and humor. Anytime we are laughing, we are in Light.

The box or chest

When you notice a box or chest floating around in etheric space, or if a guide presents you with a box or chest, the correct action is to open it. There will almost always be something inside, and in most cases, what is inside will not be a generic or common object, but something that is specific to you. For example, you may be presented with a box, and when you open it, inside you may find a memory that is meaningful to you which provides clear guidance on whatever you are working on. Or, you may be presented with a box, and inside you will find the solution to a problem—the solution may be a thought or a knowing, instead of another object. Or, you may be presented with a chest, and inside you will find your mother's necklace—and this will have a clear meaning to you. The idea is, that boxes and chests contain answers and solutions to whatever we are currently working on or confused about.

The book

The book received as an object or gift is not usually related to the "big" book of Akashic Records. This book is smaller—its symbolic meaning is that you are meant to write, to read or to research. If you receive a book, you will know right away if you are meant to see it as a symbol of your own journey as a writer, reader or researcher, or if you are meant to open it, and see if there is a simple message inside. I have received this image both ways—as a stack of books, which symbolized that my life path was to write many books, and as a book that I opened, only to see a simple sentence message written there.

The quill or pen

The quill often looks like a feather—and because this is a symbol from ancient times, we sometimes cannot recognize it. We think

Gifts and Objects 103

"oh, a feather" and may take a moment to recognize that it is actually a quill pen, the tool of the ancient scribe. We may also receive a pen. Both of these are instruments of writing, and the message is to write—you might write a book, but you just as easily might write someone a letter or an email. If you receive a quill or pen as you are transitioning to your journey, bring it with you. It is a reminder to communicate in writing, in your real life.

The ball or orb

The ball or orb is a condensed sphere of energy. For example, if you see a golden ball, it may present as a ball made of gold—but it is also an orb of condensed golden energy. A ball or orb may be any color—usually the colors relate to the chakra colors, which are energetic signatures for vibrational levels. Because an orb is a sphere of condensed energy, it is usually meant for healing or protection. Orbs often shape shift and change size. Tuck it into your pocket now, and don't be surprised if it expands in size later.

The ring

A ring may be a sign of commitment or level of consciousness. For example, in Catholic tradition, the Pope wears a ring—this ring portrays the Pope's commitment to God, and also the elevated status of the Pope's understanding. If you are given a ring, the meanings are similar—you may be asked to commit to your understanding of the Universe, or you may be shown that you have reached a particular level of understanding. Sometimes too, the ring means partnership or marriage—especially if this is a question that you are working on in your life.

The sword

A sword may be a symbol of protection on your journey. However, more commonly when presented with a sword or a knife you will be asked to cut energetic cording between you and another person, or between you and a situation—to end relationships or ways of being. There is nothing to know or do—if you are presented with a sword, you will be shown exactly what to do, or the guides will do it for you.

The staff

The staff—a large walking stick—is to support you on your journey, or to let you know that you will begin a new journey in your current life. This does not mean travel. These journeys are internal—emotional and spiritual. Sometimes, the staff will show up and you are meant to use it during a new journey into the etheric realm, such as when visiting a new portal. Other times, the staff will show up and you will begin a new journey—emotional and spiritual—in your earth life.

The cloak

The cloak is a gift of transformation—if you put it on you can become invisible, or it can also become a portal, whisking you to a new place. If you receive a cloak while journeying, you can use it later in your earth life, such as to become invisible in a crowd. Simply think of the cloak, and you will bring forth its powers— you will become energetically invisible, even though you remain in physical form. A cloak may also be used as a portal—to shift from one place to another. You will not do this alone, a guide will always accompany you.

Personal gifts

There are many other gifts and objects you may receive. The above list simply notes those gifts that are common to many people— they show up consistently in journeying by people of all ages and backgrounds. They are gifts that have meaning for the collective soul—arriving from our collective knowing.

It may surprise you that these gifts or objects seem like something out of a fairy tale. But remember—fairy tales came into being first as oral tradition and then later when people became literate. The form of fairy tales we know originated in the 1700s, but the tales and stories originated much, much earlier. Do our journeys contain fairy tales now because we have heard them from childhood—or did fairy tales come into being because this is what we have seen over thousands of years of journeying?

I believe it is the latter. We are a journeying people, because we are souls. We are consistently—no matter the time, place, civilization or culture—finding ways to journey. We journey in meditations, in prayer, in wandering, in dreaming—and this is the language the Universe continually communicates to us with. It is the language of symbol, of metaphor, of dream.

As souls, we exist in the waking dream: one part of us in the liminal world, the other part of us touching down briefly, from time to time, into our human experience.

Meditation: Receiving Gifts and Objects

Gifts and objects show up either as you transition into a portal, or as part of the journey itself. In other words, you may receive a gift or object right as you start your meditation, or again later when you are deep into your journey.

The process for working with gifts and objects is very simple.

First, if an object shows up at the very start of your meditation, this object is probably neutral and you are simply meant to interact with it. This is very easy! You will know exactly what to do if you are presented with an object. If it's a cup, drink from it. If it's a ring, put it on. And so on. Think of this as an energy booster or vibrational lifter for your meditation. It's a way the Universe is helping you align with the correct vibrational level you need.

One the other hand, if you have already moved into your meditation and have met a guide, objects will now be symbolically important. Remember to watch for and notice objects. Sometimes they will get presented to you quite clearly, but other times objects are quite subtle, and if you don't remember to notice them, you may miss them.

For example, if you are in the middle of your journey, and you only look forward, you may miss the acorn at your feet. When you are journeying always remember to notice what is small, subtle or just slipping past your cognizance. A way to do this is to ask questions such as "Is there an object for me to notice?" or "Is there something small I should see?"

For all objects—neutral or meaningful—if an object shows up, interact with it. For example, if you notice a cup or goblet, drink from it. If you receive a box, open it. If you receive a ring, put it on. If you receive a sword, ask how to use it. If you receive a cape, ask what it does, And so on. It's very easy—and you will know instinctively and intuitively what to do, as you are in your journey.

Finally, if you receive an object from the list previously noted, that's great. You can use that list to help you interpret the meaning. However, if you receive an object that is personal to you, work with that personal interpretation. For example, if you receive your grandmother's wedding ring from a guide, this might have meaning to you about your grandmother, about your own marriage if you are married, or about getting married, or something else that makes sense to you from your own personal memory, past, life experiences and associations.

Trust that whatever comes to mind for you, is how you should interpret this personal object. The Universes uses what we know as collective soul, and what we also know from our personal life experience in this lifetime. The meaning will be clear to you, and you can trust what you receive.

If the meaning is not clear (and yes, meaning may not be crystal clear when you are first starting to journey) just keep practicing. Over several meditations and over the course of time, as you begin to journey as a spiritual practice, you will begin to see how the pattern is unfolding—how the Universe is providing consistent information that will guide you, and how the pattern is something that will begin to take shape and make sense to you. The more you practice, the further you will get in your understanding—you will learn how soul language works, and you will be able to speak it fluently over time.

Let's try it now.

Simply follow along the instructions here, and you will receive an object as you enter meditation and/or you will meet a guide who will provide you with a symbolic gift.

1. Find a quiet place where you can relax, and where you will not be interrupted. Sit in a way that's comfortable to you. Close your eyes, and breathe in through the nose, and out through the mouth for at least three cycles. You will begin to feel floaty, as if you are drifting.

2. Continue breathing in through the nose and out through the mouth in a natural way. Begin to pay attention to the vibration in the air in the room, the air on your skin. Begin to notice density of energies clustered in the room, on the ceiling, in a corner or elsewhere.

3. Returning into your mind's eye, imagine that there is a step that you will step up onto; we will call this step level one, the vibration of peace and tranquility. Notice what this step looks like, what it is made of. Step up onto this level.

4. Imagine there is a second step; we will call this step level two, the vibration of love and light. Notice what this step looks like, what it is made of. Step up onto this level.

5. As you look around from where you are on the second step, you may notice that a neutral object is flying around. There may be a cup or goblet, a bowl, an insect, a flower, a pixie or fairy, or something else. This is a neutral object—a kind of energy booster for your journey. Interact with it in the obvious way; i.e., if it's a cup, drink from it, etc. If you don't receive an object, this is okay too. Just continue on.

6. Now from where you are on the second step, you can see that there is another space opening up and revealing itself to you. Step into this space. For most of you, this will be the open meadow we visited last time. A neutral space to begin a journey. However, if you go somewhere else, this is okay too. Just go there.

7. A guide will join you. This may be a guide you recognize, or a guide that is new to you. Either way is fine. Ask your guide a question that is on your mind, and ask to receive an object that symbolizes this question. For example, you may ask in this way "can you show me an object that provides an answer to my question of....?"

8. Your guide will show you an object. Usually this is in his or her hands. Notice the object, and then receive it from the guide. Allow all the symbolism and emotion of this object to flood into you all at once. For example, if you receive a cloak, you will also allow yourself to receive the full symbolic meaning of this object as it relates to your question, and you will also receive the full emotional content, including healing, that relates to this object for you. Let it all flood in all at once.

9. When you have fully received this object, ask a few more questions of your guide. I would limit yourself to three questions in one session. Go ahead now, and ask your guide a second question and receive a second object.

10. When you're ready, ask your guide a third question and receive a third object.

11. When you're complete, say thank you to your guide and find the second step of love and light. Step down onto it. Find the first step of peace and tranquility. Step down onto it. Come back to this reality by counting yourself back from 10 to 1, and opening your eyes.

As soon as you are able, journal the three question(s) you asked and the three object(s) you received. Explore what the object(s) mean to you, and how they answered your questions.

Accelerating your abilities

If you practice daily, you will quickly accelerate your abilities. Very soon, you will be able to enter in, ask a question and receive a gift that is a symbolic answer. A short time after that, you will no longer need to formally enter in every time you have a question—you will simply relax, ask the question and the gift will appear as a symbol. Sometime after that, you will simply think the question and you will know the answer—you will have the ability to have direct knowing.

Daily practice—continually deep immersion in the Divine realms via soul travel—will bring you to direct knowing, a state in which you experience Oneness at such a level that all is known to you as soul. This level of understanding is life changing.

Lesson 7

Dreamland

Dreams are not meditations. But dreams are also soul travel.

In dreamland, you will visit the same common portals as you do in meditation. You may also astral project to different places and times. And you may pre-see places that you will visit soon—in the next day, week or months.

I dream every night, and over the years, my dreams have become more vivid than ever.

It's usual for me to wake in the hours of *amrit vela*, the time when the veil between worlds is especially thin. It is a time of vulnerability—I am in bed, in the dark, with the stars and sometimes the moon bright in the sky—and I sense my own mortality, and my own vastness, and my own suffering, and it is an ideal time to meditate. This has become my practice when I wake up, and it's become something I look forward to. It feels like a magical time, when everything is open and it is very easy to cross the veil into other dimensions. I don't consider this a problem,

such as insomnia—my belief is that I am being awakened for my
sadhana—my spiritual practice—at the time when the rest of the
world is sleeping, and I am most open to the Universe and its
guidance.

During this time I meditate, I ask the Universe to guide me on
whatever I am meant to understand. For example, last night, a hot
August night when the temperature was still high all night, I was
accompanied by the steady mantra of crickets in chorus—it was
loud, it was many beings, and so I meditated to their sound, and
I was grateful to be awake listening to them.

After an hour or so, I drifted back into sleep.

And here is where this early morning waking becomes tricky
for me.

The meditation is always beautiful—I journey, I travel, I
receive guidance, I receive understanding for my direction in
the coming days, months. I am given guidance on what to do. I
receive comfort and relief from suffering. Often, I feel white light
pouring into my crown chakra and flooding my body, as a kind of
healing. So obviously, this is a very profound time.

But after the meditation—the time when I fall asleep the
second time—I experience incredibly intense dreams. They are
not nightmares. But they are vivid, intense visions of a symbolic
and emotional nature. They are often prophetic, and they often
contain a spiritual lesson.

Times of natural disasters are trying. At the time of this writing
we have been experiencing huge hurricanes in the Caribbean, and
the dreams are of water, of wind, of people suffering. This dream is
is not a nightmare—it is actually a kind of astral traveling to where
this collective suffering is happening. I am not the only one who
feels this—as collective soul, we all do.

During other times of violence that capture global attention,
the dreams are also intense. This is not just my sole anxiety. I
would gather that we are all dreaming the same dream in those
moments—dreams of darkness, and wanting to be free from that
darkness. Again, as collective soul, we all feel everything together.

Yet, other dreams are not about collective soul or collective experience. Many times, the Universe is simply trying to reach each of us personally, to provide us with the soul lesson we are ready to learn.

For example, I recently dreamt that I was at a party—a fancy party, the kind you might think of when imagining a party in Hollywood. I have never been to a party like this, and probably never will. In the dream, I went into a bedroom where everyone's coats and purses were piled on the bed. When I located my own purse, it felt suspiciously light. I looked inside and saw my wallet had been stripped clean. Everything was gone! Cash, driver's license, credit card, cell phone, car keys. Everything was gone!

In the dream, I panicked—how could I have been so dumb, to leave my identities where anyone could steal them?

And then, something shifted. Somehow in my dream, I realized that even though I had lost my identities, I had not lost my true identity. My identities, as represented by all these tokens of identities in the "real" world—cash, driver's license, credit card, cell phone, car keys—could not be lost.

I remained who I was, without any of those. I was still a soul. I had only lost my false identities—and the Universe was clearly telling me to recognize this. The true identity—that of knowing myself as soul—could not be lost.

What is infinite can never be lost.

It is so easy in this modern life to become attached to our various identities. But if we lose them—if we lose our job, or a relationship, for example—we do not go away.

We remain as consciousness, as soul being.

This is just one example of how dreams work symbolically, metaphorically, archetypally, emotionally, to show us what soul lessons we are working on. We'll talk more about dreams later, but for now it is useful to remember that our dreaming life—a portal we enter without knowing how we enter into it—always reinforces what we are learning in our waking life. In meditation, in dreams, in our everyday experiences, the Universe is always working with us on our path of soul growth and expansion.

Part Five

The Akashic Records

Lesson 8

The Akashic Records

When most people talk about the Akashic Records, they are referring to the specific portals of:

- The white building
- The Book of Knowledge
- The Library
- The Viewing Room
- The Viewing Vista

However, it can be useful to understand that the Akashic Records are not limited to just these places. In fact, everywhere we go in the etheric realms is the Akashic Records, as this is just another name for collective soul, collective consciousness, unified field, Universe, Divine, God, One.

The Akashic Records is another name for the Divine realms. There are so many different names for Oneness, the Universe, the ineffable energy of everything, and the exact name for this doesn't matter. What does matter is that we, as souls, intentionally connect to the Oneness that is also us, so that we can be infused and supported by this Divine energy.

However, by calling this Divine portal the "Akashic Records" and by being able to break this concept down into specific portals within portals, it becomes easy for us to journey in these spaces. It can be hard for the human mind to "travel in the Universe," as this is such a vast concept—how do we do this, where do we go? Whereas if we are advised to "go visit The Book of Knowledge," it is easier for our consciousness to find the pathway there. Our human self likes specific and manageable tasks, even when we are meditating and journeying. Thus, working in the paradigm of the Akashic Records—even though we are really journeying in the vast Universe—can be very useful as a tool for soul travel.

Let's take a brief look at some of the common portals in the Akashic Records. Later, we'll journey to each of them so you can see what that's like.

The Book of Knowledge

The Book of Knowledge is a huge book that contains all of the knowledge of you as a soul—every single thing about you, in all lifetimes past, present and future. Most people see this as a gigantic book that contains ornate, colorful pictures and ancient text. You usually cannot read the text, but you can relate to it in telepathy. The pictures are smaller portals that can be "entered into"—you can drop yourself into a picture, and become transported into the reality that is depicted in the picture.

The Library

The Library contains all of the knowledge of the Universe—it is an infinite collection of all Books of Knowledge. Most people see the Library as a long room with library tables and books shelved floor to ceiling. It may seem difficult to know which book to choose, but a guide will appear to show you the book you are meant to look at. You can access most of the books, but some won't be available to you. My belief is that as souls, we can only access what we can understand. In any case, your guide will assist you in working in the Library.

The Viewing Window

The Viewing Window looks like the large windows at a zoo, where you can watch animals in their habitat. These windows show us scenes from our past, present and future lives, often with us in the scene. Your guide will assist you in working with The Viewing Windows.

The Viewing Vista

The Viewing Vista is a vista point on a mountain or hill that you are shown by a guide. Initially, the vista is cloud-covered or otherwise obscured. Then it clears, and a view or scene is revealed below. Sometimes, you will see a scene that immediately shows you an answer to your question. Other times, you will see a village or town. Often you fly with the Guide or are transported into the scene below; for example, you might fly into a town and explore the buildings and rooms that are there.

I have found that The Viewing Vista and the town or village that it often reveals, is a place of timelessness. It feels both ancient and futuristic, familiar and new at the same time. For example, I often visit a village that looks like ancient Egypt or some town out of Star Wars. And yet inside this very ancient town, there are all kinds of magical and futuristic thing: cups with bubbling liquid, magical wands, flying objects, and so forth. It is not a place I know, and yet I know it completely. As if my soul has lived there many time before.

Let's go a little deeper as we explore how to work with each of these portals in the Akashic Records.

Lesson 9

The Book of Knowledge

The Book of Knowledge is the book of your soul, specifically. Each of us has a unique, personal Book of Knowledge in the Akashic Records, and this contains the history of our soul in all of our lifetimes, in every moment of our consciousness in all times and dimensions.

Everything you have ever experienced, thought, imagined, said, done, perceived—your entire experience as a soul—past, present and future lives—is contained in The Book of Knowledge.

So, if you want to know something about yourself, this is the place to go!

Remember, The Book of Knowledge is not really some giant book floating in space! It is a portal, or a dimension, or both. That means that it is a journeying destination and also a journeying tool—it provides a symbolic, metaphoric, emotional and energetic way of receiving information. When we head into the particular portal that is The Book of Knowledge in The Akashic Records, we are really heading into a dimensional field where we can access information that relates to our own experience as souls, and where we can easily understand that information.

You can think of The Book of Knowledge as a book if you like. I certainly do. On the one hand, I'm aware it's a portal, a dimension. On the other hand, I also know it is easier for me to work with the information if I just think "I'm looking in a big book."

Most of us are quite familiar with books—we know how to read them, flip through them, browse them. Again, The Book of Knowledge is not a physical book. It's a portal, an energy field or dimension that we can visit and work within. But, it's got the same rules as a physical book—writing, illustrations, photos, pages, a front and back, a start and finish. The rules are what allow us to navigate this portal so easily.

Remember: everything is etheric, in this work. We are traveling beyond the physical and earthly into the etheric realms. The Universe gives us tools which have rules, qualities and characteristics we understand, so we can work with these tools easily.

Thus, The Book of Knowledge has a few rules we'll want to pay attention to.

First, it is an energetic book, which means it has pages that can be turned. You can turn pages front to back, or you can start at the back and work frontwards. You can flip to a random page. You can go back to page you looked at earlier. You can work from the table of contents, and select a page to go to that way. You navigate The Book of Knowledge as you would a physical book.

Second, it is a book with text. Some people will see text that is very ornate—the kind of ornate lettering that monks scribed long ago. Others will see ancient script, or writing in other languages. Some will see ordinary, nondescript text. Sometimes The Book will change—one day it's ornate, the next it's plain and so forth. Sometimes the text will seem alive—it will move or seem to jump on the page. Sometimes it will seem to speak or be audible, as if the text has become telepathy. All of this is normal, and may change every time you visit The Book of Knowledge.

Remember, this is a book that contains all information about your soul. If it changes, that is because there is new information that you are meant to receive for your soul growth now.

Third, the Book has images. Sometimes these are illustrations, sometimes photos, sometimes moving illustrations and sometimes movies. Again, what you experience will change each time you visit. For example, you might see an illustration of an ancient family tree, which will direct you to a branch on the family tree that will bring back a memory for you of a person you are meant to think of. That's an example of how an illustration might work—it will help you remember or know what you are meant to pay attention to. Or, you might see an image that will turn into a movie, and you will be able to watch this movie-embedded-in-the-Book. You might also even find that you are able to open a page of the Book with a movie, watch the movie for a while, then enter into a movie and become part of the scene that is happening, and then come back out and keep reviewing the book.

The Book is a tool to help you see and understand more. It is a living Book, always changing, different every time you work with it.

Finally, if you only decided to work with the Akashic Records using the Book, this would provide you with an incredible amount of information. Some people do their practices this way, and it is quite a compelling way to work. If you love the Book, work with it daily. There is no end to the information that will be revealed.

Let's take a quick visit to The Book of Knowledge now.

Meditation: Book of Knowledge

I find it is useful to have a question to ask when you are working with The Book of Knowledge. After all, this is the book that contains all the information about your soul. So, it makes sense that we might want to ask specific questions.

For this meditation, we will ask about your soul's destiny. Not just in this lifetime, but in all your lifetimes.

1.   Find a quiet spot where you can have some privacy. Close your eyes.

2.   Breathe in through the nose, out through the mouth. Repeat this several times, until you feel relaxed.

3.   Begin to go up the two steps we have used before: Step One, peace and tranquility. Step Two, love and light. You will arrive in the dimension where it is easiest for you to connect with the guides, and for the guides to communicate with you.

4.   This time, in the distance you will notice a large building. Sometimes it will have columns, or look like a large library, or look like a large museum. It's often white or pale. Walk or move or float toward this building. A guide will join you.

5.   Enter the building. This is the Akashic Records. Some people notice a large library setting, with long tables and books, and other souls studying the books. Others see bookcases. Others go to areas where there are large viewing windows that display scenes from your lifetimes. Others see other things.

6.   Your guide will take you to a place where you will see large book. This is The Book of Knowledge. You may notice that the book is very large: an ancient tome, filled with lavish illustrations and text. Open the book, or notice where it is already opened to. You may or may not be able to see the text or illustration clearly, or you may find that you can "sense" what is there.

7.   The question for this meditation is "What is my soul's destiny in this and all lifetimes?" Ask this question now.

8.   If you are directed to observe text, see what it says. There may be message for you. If you are directed to work with images, notice what you see. You may notice images that start to move or morph, so that you can enter into the image. For example, if you see an image of a small hut, you may notice that you can enter this image and suddenly are walking up to a small hut.

9.   Notice how the text or image answers your question. Your soul's destiny may be focused on one understanding. As a soul, you continue the same destiny over many lifetimes, such as "you are a healer" or "you are a teacher" or whatever it is for you. This destiny will likely be quite familiar to you; it won't be a surprise. This knowledge will help you to understand and have courage to go forth with your destiny in this lifetime.

10. When you're ready, come back to this reality—travel down the steps and travel back into your body.

11. Journal on what you experienced.

For your journal

1.   What happened during the meditation?

2.   What was revealed to you?

3.   What is your soul's destiny in this lifetime?

4.   How did this revelation help you?

Lesson 10

The Akashic Library

As a child, I was a voracious reader. I was taken to the public library once a week and allowed to choose whatever books I liked; there were no restrictions on what I was allowed to read.

Of course, the librarians steered me toward whatever children's book was recommended at that time, but I didn't gravitate to that. Mostly, I read books on religion, which was both an odd interest and an early sign of my fascination with spirituality. It was an early, peculiar interest that signaled an awareness of my soul path, my destiny in this lifetime. I am still interested in books on spirituality, as I was back then. But what also stayed with me, was a very clear understanding of how to explore a library. How to locate the books you might be interested in. How to find books you thought you never would be interested in—but then you were. How to wander among the stacks and allow a book to leap out to you—sometimes literally falling on the floor in front of your feet—as the Universe directed you synchronistically to your next piece of information.

This is how it also works in The Akashic Library. We will be directed, by the Universe to the exact books we are meant to read. There are no restrictions, save for the understanding of our soul. In other words, we can read whatever books in the Library that we can understand—books that are beyond our comprehension will not be available to us. In this same way, books that we long to read, but that don't really concern us—for example, if you had a toxic relationship with an ex, and now want to read their book in The Akashic Library, the Universe may say "that's not your concern" and this book may be unavailable to you.

Trust that whatever you are meant to read, you will be able to read. Trust also that you will be pointed to the exact books and information that is most useful for your soul growth now.

The Akashic Library works a little differently than The Book of Knowledge. For most people, it appears like an old-fashioned library, with long tables for studying, and tall stacks of books.

At first you might think this sounds a lot like the library in *Harry Potter*—and it is true, the people who created and designed that library for books and movies were definitely in connection with the archetype of library we see in collective soul. But there is more to the Library you'll experience, than in the Harry Potter library. Your Library is much more interactive, vaster and more magical.

Aside from books, there are other things that people notice in the Library. Some people notice animals in the Library, such as owls flying around. However, owls are just one example—there seems to be a lot of animal activity of all kinds. These are spirit animals, and may guide you to resources you did not know you were looking for.

There may be other beings in the stacks as well—either the guides of The Akashic Library, or other souls who are also browsing the Library (both departed and living), and also other beings who may be guides you will receive direction from. For example, it's common to see guides in The Akashic Library—they may bring you books, or give you directions, or direct you in other ways.

It would not be unusual to see a living person you know, browsing in the stacks. You might notice what they are looking for, and you may have some communication with them. It would also not be unusual for you to see a departed person you know, browsing in the stacks. You might notice what they are looking for, and you might even notice that you and the departed spirit are searching for the same book. It would also not be unusual for you to see an elf (for example) in the stacks, who hands you a book you are meant to look at—that kind of thing.

The stacks are not static—they may appear organized, but as you walk through them you may find the Library opens up to more rooms leading to more rooms. The ceilings may become taller, the shelves rise up. There may be strange spherical or pyramid shapes floating around—these might remind you of sacred geometry, or other symbols that have meaning for you. If you don't know what they mean, there may be the sense that you should know what they mean, or you once understood them, or that you deeply long to understand them.

Finally, the books themselves will act differently. There may be books that come forward on the shelves as you walk by or that seem to be pulling away from you. A book may leap out at you, fly toward you, or fall into your hand.

And, the books will be different than your own personal Book of Knowledge. For example, when you open The Book of Knowledge, you will be able to flip forward, back, look around, etc. However, when you pull a book from The Akashic Library, you may only be able to read one sentence or paragraph, or turn to one particular page. There may be limits or restrictions, so that you can't read all of a book, just the part you are meant to read.

Meditation: The Akashic Library

I find it is useful to have a question to ask when working with The Akashic Library. After all, this is the library that contains all the information of the Universe. So, it makes sense that we might want to ask specific questions.

However, sometimes we also just want to know what the Universe wants us to most know. So, you can enter in with no question, as we'll do here. Or you can hold a particular question in your mind.

Let's try it now.

1. Find a quiet spot where you can have some privacy. Close your eyes.

2. Breathe in through the nose, out through the mouth. Repeat this several times, until you feel relaxed.

3. Begin to go up the two steps we have used before: Step One, peace and tranquility. Step Two, love and light. You will arrive in the dimension where it is easiest for you to connect with the guides, and for the guides to communicate with you.

4. This time, in the distance you will notice a large building. Sometimes it will have columns, or look like a large library, or look like a large museum. It's often white or pale. Walk or move or float toward this building. A guide will join you.

5. Enter the building. This is the Akashic Records. Some people notice a large library setting, with long tables and books. Notice what you notice.

6. For this meditation, we will ask the Universe to provide you with the message that you are meant to hear right now—it is a message you need to hear clearly, and one that you may not have heard clearly before now, or that you may have resisted hearing in the past. Hold this intention in your mind: you are asking the Universe to provide you with the message you most need to hear.

7. As you hold this intention, start looking around. Do you notice any other souls in the area, such as guides, departed or people you know who are current living? If you feel

drawn to interact with them, please do so now. They may have a book or message for you, or lead you somewhere, or something else.

8.   Do you notice any other beings in the area, such as spirit animals or elemental beings? If you feel drawn to interact with them, please do so now. They may have a book or message for you, or lead you somewhere, or something else.

9.   You will be drawn to a stack of books where the book(s) you are meant to look at are waiting for you. As you near the stack, notice what books seem to want you to notice them. They may be moving, or fall toward you, or something else.

10. When you have found the book that you are drawn to, open it and see what message is there for you. You may receive one line of text that you read almost as a telepathy—it may not be like reading as you are used to, it may be as if you can sense the meaning as you look at it. If the text is written in an ancient script, for example, just ask to sense or know the messages—even if you don't speak or can't read that language, you will be able to see it. If you see an illustration or photo, notice what that means to you. If you're not sure what it means (i.e., if you open the book to a picture of a symbol you are not familiar with) ask the Universe to make this meaning clear to you.

11. As you receive the message from the book, this will relate to something you are working on, or something you "need to hear."

12. If you're drawn to look at more books, continue exploring the stacks until you are drawn to other books. Most people won't explore more than three books in a journey, as this is plenty of information to receive. For your second and/ or third books, you may choose to ask specific questions of your choosing.

13. If anything else needs to happen, it will. Just notice everything in this space and you will be drawn to whatever information you need. If you seem to be restricted from some information, no worries. The Universe will provide you with the answers you are ready for and the answers that are yours to know at this time in your life.

14. When you're ready, come back to this reality—travel down the steps and travel back into your body.

15. Journal on what you experienced.

For your journal

1. What did you notice or observe in The Akashic Library?

2. Did you notice any other souls, beings or animals?

3. What books did you receive?

4. What messages did you read in the book(s)?

5. What did you learn?

Lesson 11

The Viewing Window

The Viewing Window is a portal or dimension in the Akashic Records where you can have the experience of watching a scene play out. This may occur in the past, such as you may see a scene of yourself as a child in a situation that you remember, or that you have forgotten. You may see yourself a year ago, in a situation that you remember, or that you have forgotten. You can see multiple scenes in your lifetime.

For those of you who have worked with the clairvoyant rose as I teach it, you have also come across the idea of the Viewing Screen. They are very similar tools for gathering intuitive and spiritual information. The way to look at it is that the Viewing Screen is a smaller visioning portal that hovers in front of your third eye; you often use it to put questions "up" on it, to see how the answer unfolds. You either use it with a clairvoyant rose, or you use it for straight visioning.

The difference with The Viewing Window is that you won't use a rose, and you won't "put things up." They will be waiting for you to watch, as if you are watching a movie of yourself that is dimensional and real, and that you can also enter into. There is no clairvoyant rose, because you are seeing the scene play out in front of you, whether you are seeing a memory from the past or a past life or something from the future.

Both the Viewing Screen and Viewing Window are tools for visioning.

The Viewing Window is something that you can control to some extent. For example, you can request to look at a particular memory, or work your way through several memories over time. You can look at the far past, you can look at the recent past, and you can flip back and forth.

You can look at things "big picture" such as seeing the scene from far away, or from a wide angle. Or you might notice the smallest little detail. You can view the screen from outside The Viewing Window, or you can enter into the scene and be a part of it.

You can also control the speed or rate at which you are receiving information. For example, if a lot of visual information is coming very quickly, or you simply want to look at part of the scene in more detail, you can simply ask The Viewing Window to pause so you can look more closely. For those of you who have a lot of experience with journeying, this will be very familiar. If you haven't journeyed a lot, you can start practicing and trying this out as you work with The Viewing Window. Ask it to speed up, slow down, zoom in, zoom out, focus on something, focus on something else—you can control what you are receiving.

It is common to have emotion and understanding while you are using The Viewing Window. You will have full heart understanding for whatever you see before you. You understand now what you did not understand at the time you were in that particular experience.

The Viewing Window is especially useful when you use it to work through memories—either remembered or forgotten.

Remembering events can help us see the significant events that moved you from one experience to another.

The Universe is always nudging and guiding us into position, creating synchronistic convergences that move you into position so that you can work on your soul lessons. As an example of how the Universe nudges us, let's say you get a new job, and because of this you meet the person you will marry, and because of this you move to another state, and because of this, you start working in a different field which leads you to your life's work: all of these outcomes stem from the convergence of getting a new job. The Universe has nudged you on this path, not randomly, but by design, to help you learn your soul lessons.

Or, you might get in a car accident, and because of this you lose your job, and lose your home, and you have no choice but to move in with a relative in cramped quarters for several years. In this way, with this convergence of the accident, your life is changed: the Universe creates the convergence or the event, in order to nudge you to a position where you will be available to learn soul lessons.

The first example might be seen as "positive" and the second example as "negative" but in truth, everything just is as it is.

We don't know where everything is leading us. If you have been on this planet a few decades or so, you know that there are ups and downs, high points and low points, and these are all part of life—necessary to help us understand and grow.

There is no judgment about what kind of lessons you're learning: all souls are on the path. "Good" things don't happen to "good" people, and "bad" things don't happen to "bad" people. Sometimes we need to learn via "positive" lessons. Sometimes we need to learn via "negative" lessons. All kinds of things happen to all kinds of people.

If you were raised on the idea of original sin, or the concept that if you are "good" and "follow the rules" that your life will be simple and easy—you will benefit if you let that idea go. The Universe doesn't care about "good." The Universe doesn't care if you "follow the rules."

The Universe is only interested in your expansion as a soul, and sometimes this requires us to have experiences that are bad and break all the rules. As souls, we will have many experiences in many lifetimes: one lifetime we're a pirate terrorizing the high seas, the next lifetime we're a gentle grandma who knits for charity. Which is "better"? Which is "worse"?

The Viewing Window helps us look back at our memories and experience them in a new way—we can see them as moments in time when the Universe nudged us to a new position, interfered on our behalf, helped to learn a soul lesson, or expanded in some way. Even if we were not particularly conscious when we had the experience the first time, as we review the memory in The Viewing Window, we can now appreciate the experience in a new way. We can understand more, or we can understand entirely, why this part of our life happened.

People talk about receiving a "piece of the puzzle" when they do journeying, and this is what the Viewing Screen is very good for—for helping us retrieve a piece of the puzzle, so that we understand more about our experience in this life; why we went through what we did, how the Universe helped us, and what we have learned from this.

Again, The Viewing Window allows us to relive and review significant moments in this lifetime, so that we realize the grand scheme of the Universe at work in our lives. When we work with The Viewing Window, we are able to see and appreciate moments and memories that we've forgotten, or memories that we've forgotten, and understand why they were important to us and how they changed the course of our lives.

Finally, it is true that we can also use The Viewing Window to visit past and future lives, but in general, I find it is more useful and easier to use other tools when we are looking at our past or future lifetimes, especially the Tree of Life and the River. We'll cover those portals later on.

So, what does a Viewing Window look like? Most people will experience The Viewing Window as a large floor to ceiling window in the Akashic Records building. You stand in front of it, and as you watch as you are shown parts of your life.

Although you can usually enter into the scene that is displayed in front of you, but there is still a sense of being the observer. You are either viewing the scene from behind The Viewing Window, or if you have entered into the scene, you still retain the detachment of being the observer. You will likely feel heart opening and emotion as you work with the Viewing Screen, but you will also have this sense of being witness—you are there, but you are aware that you are witnessing, not experiencing.

Meditation: Viewing Window

The Viewing Window helps you revisit important, perhaps even crucial conjunctures in your lifetime and see them as they happened. At the time, you might not have understood they were important, or why they were important or what they were setting in motion. But now, as you see them in The Viewing Window, you get to get be the fly on the wall and view yourself outside of the perspective of "you." You get to understand why this particular event was so meaningful—what it meant, what it set in motion, what it healed, what it activated, what it created.

Let's try it now.

1.   Find a quiet spot where you can have some privacy. Close your eyes.

2.   Breathe in through the nose, out through the mouth. Repeat this several times, until you feel relaxed.

3.   Begin to go up the two steps we have used before: Step One, peace and tranquility. Step Two, love and light. You will arrive in the dimension where it is easiest for you to connect with the guides, and for the guides to communicate with you.

4.   This time, in the distance you will notice a large building. Sometimes it will have columns, or look like a large library, or look like a large museum. It's often white or pale. Walk or move or float toward this building. A guide will join you.

5.   Enter the building. This is the Akashic Records. This time, you will notice a room or rooms usually to the right, which are where The Viewing Windows are located. It will be normal for you to see other guides and other souls milling about in this journey. However, you will be taken to a place where you can work with your own Viewing Window.

6.   Most people see The Viewing Window as a floor to ceiling window; it is an observatory window. Notice how it appears to you, and take a glance and notice which scene you are first seeing.

7.   For this meditation, we will ask the Universe to take you to a memory that will unlock something you have been working on for a while—it will be a "piece of the puzzle." One of the normal ways the Universe will do this, is by allowing a number to pop into your mind that is an age, such as 7 or 14 or 23. Or any number. If you have the sense of a number popping into your mind, this may be an age where you will find the memory you are meant to view.

8.   Observe The Viewing Window, and notice what begins to take shape. Do you see a scene of yourself at a particular age? Where are you? What do you look like? Is anyone with you? What are you doing? As you observe more deeply, try to determine if this is a scene that you remember, or if is a memory that you've forgotten.

9.   Notice the emotions that are starting to come up as you observe or interact with this memory. If you feel emotion,

allow it to come. If you don't feel emotion, this is okay too. Just notice.

10.   If you feel like you want to enter the scene, do so. If you prefer to observe, this is okay too. What is happening? What have you forgotten that you are noticing now? Are there any people or objects you are meant to notice? What else?

11.   As you observe, become aware of the soul lesson you were learning during this experience of your life. How did this experience shift you into a new future? How did the Universe use this experience to nudge you in a new direction? Was this experience a crucial convergence in your life that you recognized, or was it a smaller event that you weren't aware of? What else?

12.   When you are done with that particular memory, you can either return to this reality, or if you'd like to keep going, you can ask the Universe to show you another memory at a different age, and repeat the process. After that second memory is done, you can ask for a third memory if you want. Sometimes the memories all relate to each other, sometimes they show you different parts of yourselves. Watch for patterns and understanding that tie in what you are receiving.

13.   When you're fully done, return to this reality by taking a step down from love and light, then a step down from peace and tranquility and back into this reality.

14.   Journal on what happened.

For your journal

1.   What memory were you shown in The Viewing Window?

2.   Is this something you remembered, or had you forgotten?

3. Did it bring up emotions?

4. Did it bring up understanding?

5. If you looked at more than one memory, what is the bigger pattern, message or knowing?

Lesson 12

The Vista

The Vista is an extraordinary portal outside of the Akashic Records building. Imagine that you are in a beautiful setting that contains all of the knowledge of the Universe, filled with all the guides and ascended masters, and with other souls who are there to receive that knowledge.

Now, imagine that you have browsed and studied and learned in the building, and suddenly a guide, either a guide you know or a new guide, will ask you to join them on a walk outside. While we might expect the walk to be in magical gardens or some other palatial scene, what I find is that most people experience the walk as a gently rising path uphill, with either grasses or meadow flowers on the sides of the path. It's not particularly fancy, for most people most of the time. It's just taking a walk with your guide to a vista or viewing point, and this is where the excitement begins.

When you are at this viewing point, you will be able to see what is below. A bank of clouds, a valley below, a town below, something else? As the guide shows you this place, you will feel yourself lifting off from the vista point, and traveling in the air to what is below.

Some people experience this as flying. Some people use a device such as a flying carpet or mythical being. Some travel with their guides. Some just have the sense of instant transportation. In any case, one moment you're on the vista and the next you're in the space you have just seen, and you are experiencing this place.

As an example, your guide might show you a bank of clouds, and as you pose a question in your mind, the bank of clouds will roll back to show a scene or place that contains your answer. One interesting thing about the Vista is that it never takes you to memory. It always takes you to past life, or future life, or a parallel life, or a magical life. It takes you to information that is not of this world, or not of your experience.

So, there is this wondrous fantastical aspect, which is incredibly enjoyable.

This is the place you will see mythical creatures, strange plants and animals, strange devices you have never seen before. The entire environment is different. So, this makes it very interesting to look around. There is a great deal of future seeing in the Vista experience, and this is exciting. You will be seeing things you have never seen before, and that you have never imagined.

Mostly, the Vista experience will answer very "big" questions about your soul path over many lifetimes. This usually has to do with either your life's calling—the soul contribution you are here to make in every lifetime, and continuous refrain that you will find as you explore—or the most important, karmic relationship you have with others in your primary soul cluster over many lifetimes.

Meditation: The Vista

Overall, expect a fantastical or futuristic journey if you are invited to the Vista by a guide. Remember: the walking up to the Vista point may be somewhat generic, but as always, if something catches your eye there or seems different or unusual, always take a moment to notice it.

For example, if you normally see grasses as you walk up the path, pay attention if suddenly that is made up of sunflowers. If the path is normally easy to climb, but you find you suddenly have a rock in your shoe, stop and deal with that. If the cloud bank is usually fluffy, but this time it is ominous rainclouds and flashing lightning, stop and ask why.

Everything in a psychic journey is important, and there is always something to notice. Pay attention to anything unusual, unexpected or new, whenever you are journeying.

Let's try it now.

1. Find a quiet spot where you can have some privacy. Close your eyes.

2. Breathe in through the nose, out through the mouth. Repeat this several times, until you feel relaxed.

3. Begin to go up the two steps we have used before: Step One, peace and tranquility. Step Two, love and light. You will arrive in the dimension where it is easiest for you to connect with the guides, and for the guides to communicate with you.

4. This time, in the distance you will notice a large building. Sometimes it will have columns, or look like a large library, or look like a large museum. It's often white or a pale color. Walk or move or float toward this building. A guide will join you.

5. The guide will take you either through the building (the Akashic Records) or to the side of the building, where you will begin walking a gentle path up a mountain hill. Normally, it is not hard to do this walk, it is a very gentle slope upwards. If you find that it is difficult, take this as a sign to notice and ask your guide why. You will also

notice what is around the path: are you walking through flowers, scrubby grasses, rocks and so forth. Just notice.

6.   When you get to the Vista, you will see a vast cloudbank over a vast valley. As you arrive, your guide will show you that the cloudbank is driving away, so you can see clearly what is below you. You may recognize this valley by its characteristics, such as where it might be in the world, even if it is in the future. Or you might not recognize it at all.

7.   Your guide will begin to take you to the valley. This usually happens by flying. Either you will start to fly alongside your guide, or your guide will take you under his or her wing or robe, or a mythical creature will arrive to take you, or some other device such as a flying carpet or other device will show up. This is going to be very individual for each person, and this journey can be very fantastical and futuristic. Allow whatever happens to happen and don't be concerned if it seems outlandish or out of a fantasy adventure. The Universe is a magical place and we experience much we don't understand when we journey.

8.   You will fly into the valley or the town, and you will find yourself somewhere. For example, you may fly into an open window of a building in the town in the valley, and this will be a place you are meant to explore. If there are no buildings in your valley, then you will fly to the ground and see what happens.

9.   If you are in a building, notice what is around you: what types of objects, what the feeling or flavor is, what the colors are, everything. For example, one of the most common places that I go in journeying from the Vista is to a magical town that feels like ancient Morocco, except it is very futuristic. I fly into a room filled with what I believe are musical instruments or art objects, but they are not. They are meant for something else, but because

they are future objects, I am not sure. My best sense is that they are tools for moving energy or working with energy. The room is a soft peach or orange, and everything in the room, the objects, are a soft pale and pearly white. Your journey will be different, of course, but I share this so you will have an understanding of how you may experience things you don't understand, but you can still sense how they feel, and this will be enough.

10. If you are called to explore further, please do this. You may wander through a town, visit many buildings, go elsewhere, or something else. Explore and notice with your guide, until you feel complete.

11. When you're ready to return, you can either retrace your steps by flying back to the Vista, walking back to the Akashic Records, finding your way to this reality by taking a step down from love and light, then a step down from peace and tranquility and back into this reality. Or, you can simply go directly to the step of love and light, and continue down from there.

12. Journal on what happened.

For your journal

1. What were you shown in the Vista journey?

2. Was this something you have seen before or was it new?

3. What did you see that you have never seen?

4. What was the overall message of this Vista journey?

Lesson 13

The Tree of Life

The Tree of Life is found in religious and myth traditions all over the world. It is part of the Kabbalah, Christianity, Buddhism, Baha'I, Hinduism, Muslim, Paganism and Norse mythologies, to name a few. It is sometimes known as the tree of ancestors or the family tree, but it does not always relate to ancestry or family.

In spiritual journeying it is known as The Tree of Life, and it is most often understood as a portal to past lives.

A common experience of The Tree of Life is as a portal in the root system, where we descend into the roots of the tree and head down into the cavernous space below the tree, where we are able to explore past lives. We might also see many other souls here, in a crystalline cave that is filled with guides and spirit teachers.

Lesson commonly used, the branches and leaves of the tree are also portals that can take us to different realms. As you work with The Tree of Life, remember that both aspects are available: traveling down to past lives, or traveling up to other realms. Because we've already spent so much time traveling up to other realms, we'll focus on using The Tree of Life as a portal to past lives.

Understanding past lives

There is a difference between ancestry and past lives. When people start to journey back in time, they may see glimpses of their ancestors and or their past lives, and sometimes these are different and sometimes these are the same.

When you travel back in time to see your ancestors, you are dropped into times and places several generations back, and you will be visiting your bloodline, your ancestral heritage. For example, if your ancestors are from Africa, you will find yourself in those countries. If your ancestors are Celtic, you will find yourself in those countries. However, these will not be your past lives. They simply reflect your ability to journey back in time, to astrally project yourself back, and to take a look around at what was happening back then and there.

This process of projecting yourself into the past can be very interesting; however, in my experience it doesn't have a lot to teach us about your soul lessons. Remember, when you go and visit your ancestral past, you are observing or witnessing other souls, ancestor souls. However, your soul is not there. It's as if you're watching family members at a party, but you're not at the party, and they don't even know you're in the family.

So, I find that this process is interesting, but not that revealing. And, in this work we are doing spiritual journeying, we are journeying to find insight and understanding about the path of our own soul.

In past live work, we are able to see the progress of our soul, in other lifetimes that either parallel or differ from this lifetime. We aren't looking at other relatives, we're looking at our self, as a soul living in a previous lifetime. The information is much richer, and we are able to learn a lot by watching our self in previous lifetimes.

In using The Tree of Life as a past life portal, then, we are able to journey to our own past lives, and work with them as mirrors or markers of ourselves, whether we see a similar or different past life.

Let's continue, as we explore both.

Guiding past lives are past lives that mirror your present life. They are invitations to look at what you soul was dealing with then, that mirrors what your soul is dealing with now. When we know how to access our guiding past lives—our parallel past live—we can explore these experiences to understand the karma—the soul lessons—we are working on in this life.

Lesson 14

Guiding Past Lives

Of course, there are thousands of past lives. Again, *guiding* past lives are different, because they parallel or mirror this lifetime. We can ask the guides to show us a guiding past life, instead of any of our other past lives, in order to understand more about the soul lessons we're experiencing now.

Guiding past lives

When you work with a guiding past life, you'll be "you" as a soul. But your soul will be in a different body, with a different personality, in a different place and time.

There are often a lot of commonalities in a guiding past life. You'll be "you" as a soul, and you'll be working on the same lessons you're working on now. It's common to:

- Live in a similar environment

- Have a similar social status
- Have a similar personality style
- Have a similar body or health style
- Be doing similar life's work
- Be surrounded by people in your soul circle (i.e., your spouse in this lifetime is your child in the past life). Same souls, different roles.
- Be working on the same soul lessons (i.e., if you have a temper now, you may see that you had a temper then, etc.).

All of the similarities help you understand what this other person, this "you" that was you, was learning in this past lifetime.

At first, it may seem that because there are so many similarities, it's unreal. But it's not. If you were to choose to simply access a past life that was not a guiding past life for this lifetime, you would end up with thousands of possibilities that aren't remotely like the life you're living now.

We seek the guiding past life, because it helps us understand more about this lifetime.

Meditation: Parallel Past Lives

Here is the long form for a past life regression that parallels your current lifetime.

It is good to use the long form when you haven't been practicing for a while, or when you want to make sure you can go deep and gather the information you need.

This past life regression is designed to take you to a past life that is guiding past life: a lifetime that parallels or mirrors the life you are living now. Before you begin, let to go of anything anyone's ever told you about who you were in another life. Just let all go. Allow the Universe to choose, and expect to be surprised.

1. Close your eyes.

2. Breathe in through the nose, out through the mouth. Repeat this several times, until you feel very relaxed.

3. In your mind's eye, locate a large tree to work with. This can be a tree outside, or a tree that arrives as a vision.

4. Enter into a doorway you will find in the trunk or at the base of the tree. Continue down into the root system, which is likely to appear as a long dimly hallway. A guide will arrive to accompany you. Notice if this is a "generic" guide or one you work with often.

5. Continue descending down into the roots, until you find yourself in a large cavernous room that is filled with light. Notice if there are other beings there. Notice the surroundings. Look at the walls of this room, and notice that they are filled with photos, portraits, mementos, items... all things that represent all the many lifetimes that you have had. There will be thousands of these up and down the walls. All of these are you.

6. Walk toward a photo, portrait, memento or object that calls you. Don't overthink it or try to figure it out. Just let it happen. Trust that you'll naturally and easily be drawn to one. When you reach it, notice it in detail. Who is in the photo? What are they wearing? Who is in the portrait? What time are they from? Are they male or female? If you are called to a memento, use your understanding of energy and vibration to recall this object and who it belonged to.

7. Enter the photo, or the portrait. If you have a memento or object, hold onto it, and dissolve into it.

8. You will find yourself immediately in a new surrounding: the photo, portrait, memento or object is a portal. It has transported you to somewhere else. Notice the environment around you. Are you warm or cold? Is it

light or dark? Are you in the country or the city? What is the plant life like? Are there any buildings around you or in the distance?

9. Look down, and notice your hands, your feet. Feel your hair. Are you man or woman? How old? Rich or poor (if you are barefoot, you are likely poor or a peasant. If you wear a fine fabric, you are likely rich.). What else?

10. Where are you drawn to go? To a building nearby? To a town in the distance? Something else? Go there now.

11. Where do you end up? Who is there? Do you know this person in your lifetime now? What work are you doing? What is your life's work in this lifetime? Can you see the tools you use? What else do you notice?

12. Recall that your guide has come with you. Ask your guide now, to show you the soul lessons you have been learning in this lifetime. You may view an experience that lets you understand this, or you may see something, or you may have a feeling, or something else may happen. Understand this fully.

13. Look around for anything else that you are meant to see or know. You may receive an object from the guide, or be drawn to an object in this past life. Recall that all objects have meaning. For example, if a guide gives you sunflowers: How many? Are they bigger than usual? Are they healthy? Do they remind you of something or someone? Does the color correspond to a chakra? Nothing is random, generic or coincidental. Notice and understand.

14. When you are ready, you will easily find the portal to come back to the cavernous room. Go there. If there is any ceremony or ritual you are meant to do in this room, you will know that.

15. Begin to climb up the hallways through the root system, come out the tree trunk, and move your spirit-self back

into your body. Call your aura back to you, so that no parts of your soul energy are left in the past life, or anywhere else.

16. When you're ready, come back to this reality. Journal on what you experienced.

For your journal

1. Who were you in this past life?

2. What did you do? What was your life's work?

3. Who else was there? Who were you in relationship to?

4. Were you given any symbolic object?

5. What was your soul lesson?

6. How is this past life similar to your life now?

Lesson 15

More Guiding Past Lives

We've all had so many past lives! You could spend every moment of your current lifetime deep in meditation, exploring your past lives! Of course, we want to live our lives not just review the lifetimes we've already had.

However, experiencing more than one past life will provide us with more understanding.

This time, we will experience a Guiding Past Life that is not familiar. In other words, we will ask the Universe to provide us with an experience that is very different than what we experienced last week, and also very different from what we are experiencing now in this lifetime.

For example, if in your life now you are an artist, and if in last week's past life you were an artisan, you might expect that in all your past lives, you've been an artist or worked with your hands.

But this may not be so.

Or if, in your life now, you are a parent, and if in last week's past life you found yourself as part of a family, you might expect that in all your past lives, you've been experiencing family and children.

Again, this may not be so.

Maybe you have been an artist or artisan for many past lives, and even for many past lives leading up to this current one. However, during some past lives, you were not an artist or artisan. You were exploring different parts of yourself, and you had a life's calling that was different. Maybe you were an adventurer, or an explorer, or a pirate instead! Maybe you were a nurse or a caretaker or a mother.

The idea is, we do many tasks, we have many experiences during our past lives, and some past lives will be similar to this current one and others will be very different.

In general, the past lives that are most similar to now will be more recent, whereas the past lives that are most different will be many lifetimes away, but this is not always the case. The Universe is Mystery, and exploring past lives is a pioneering field. We are just learning to explore what is there. The best approach is to consider yourself an explorer in uncharted territory, and simply notice what happens while you are journeying.

For this week's past life regression, we're going to ask the Universe to provide you with a very different past life, so that you can see yourself as soul, having another experience that is vastly different from what you are experiencing now.

Recall that soul remains the same.

You are the same soul in this past life, even if what you are doing, who you are with or what you are able to understand is vastly different.

Personality can remain similar in some lifetimes—we can bring our personality with us from lifetime to lifetime. However, this isn't always the case. What is more common is for us to have less developed personalities in long-ago past lives, and as we have evolved through lifetimes, we've expanded as souls and learned how to work with our personalities a bit better. As we know, the more we understand, the more we change.

Your personality many past lives ago may have been aggressive and fearful, whereas now you have evolved to a personality that is non-violent but anxious, and then as you evolve more into other lifetimes, you will evolve to a personality that is calm and loving, and so forth.

Body can remain similar also across past lives also, but again: the more you understand, the more you experience different cultures and situations, the more your body evolves.

In general, as you move through soul lessons, you move beyond what you were struggling with. You experience soul lessons, you master them over one or many lifetimes, and you keep moving forward as a soul.

There isn't any going backward in your understanding or your expansion. Recall, we are here on a journey of soul growth. As you master soul lessons, you expand as a soul and you are given more challenging lessons, and as you master those, you expand as a soul, etc. Once you know, you know. There is no regression.

Notice that our soul lessons continually become more challenging as we expand in our understanding, but it may not look that way on paper. For example, a soul lesson you might have learned in a long-ago past life was not to be afraid of all the terrifying animals who roamed at night. That seems like a big and challenging soul lesson. Now, in this lifetime, maybe you are completely safe from all terrifying night predators, but you are facing the soul lesson of how to be happy in your life. That seems like an easier soul lesson on the surface, but as anyone living in today's culture knows, it's a very difficult soul lesson to master.

We're given the soul lessons we're ready for, and once we learn those, we move on to new, more challenging soul lessons. And yet, they are not more challenging from the outer view. Our soul lessons get more and more subtle as we expand as souls. For example, it is easy to see the leap from fear into calm. But the soul lesson of moving from joy into love is subtler, and more complex. We are given each soul lesson as we are ready. We will work on many soul lessons in a lifetime, and we have many lifetimes—in fact, as many as we need—to master any given soul lesson.

As further example, once you've learned the lesson of money karma, you begin to live in abundance, lifetime after lifetime. You no longer have to work on that lesson.

Note: this may or may not mean you're "rich." It means you've learned the lesson; you've graduated from worry and concern about money, you know how to manifest what you need, and you trust that you're always provided for.

Money is no longer your lesson... which means you're going to have time to work on whatever other, different lesson is next for you.

In this case, at the beginning of your soul's path, you might have had many lifetimes in which you were very poor. But, as you learned about abundance, this shifted. As you learned across lifetimes, you might have had a lot of ups and downs; you might have been starving, very poor, then rich, then lost everything, then rich again, then lost everything again, stabilized and so on, until you finally understood the lesson about abundance. As you cracked the code, you permanently moved into a place where abundance was no longer a lesson that you needed to learn; you'd learned it already.

Note: the soul lesson about money is: the energy of abundance is unlimited. Once you have fully mastered that lesson, you move on to something else. You don't have to repeat that lesson, because you have gained that understanding.

Or, perhaps your soul lesson is about primary relationships. In past lives you've been single, then partnered, then lost your partner, then been betrayed, on and on in all possibilities, until you finally learn the lesson of how to live with another person without strife and in joy. Many lifetimes of learning!

If you've learned this lesson, hurrah! You get new lessons to work on. If not, more experiences on relationships to come.

Note: the soul lesson about relationships is: unconditional love for self and other.

In any case... it can be very interesting to see yourself in this new Guiding Past Life, as it will shed light on lessons you've been working on in the past that you may no longer be working on now. Or it may show you something different: the Universe will decide.

Meditation: Differing Past Lives

Here is the long form for a past life regression that will show you a lifetime that is different than your current lifetime.

It is good to use the long form when you haven't been practicing for a while, or when you want to make sure you can go deep and gather the information you need.

This past life regression is designed to take you to a past life that is guiding past life that is different from your current lifetime: a lifetime that will show you something different than what you're experiencing now.

Let's try it now.

Before you begin, let to go of anything anyone's ever told you about who you were in another life. Just let it all go. Allow the Universe to choose, and expect to be surprised.

1. Close your eyes.

2. Breathe in through the nose, out through the mouth. Repeat this several times, until you feel very relaxed and possibly a little woozy.

3. In your mind's eye, locate a large tree to work with. This can be a tree outside, or a tree that arrives as a vision.

4. Enter into a doorway you will find in the trunk or at the base of the tree. Continue down into the root system, which is likely to appear as a long, dimly lit hallway.

5. A guide will arrive to accompany you. Notice if this is a "generic" guide or one you work with often.

6. Continue descending down into the roots, until you find yourself in a large cavernous room that is filled with light. Notice if there are other beings there. Notice the surroundings. Look at the walls of this room, and notice

that they are filled with photos, portraits, mementos, items ... all things that represent all the many lifetimes that you have had. There will be thousands of these up and down the walls. All of these are you.

7.   Walk toward a photo, portrait, memento or object that calls you. You'll just be drawn to one. When you reach it, notice it in detail. Who is in the photo? What are they wearing? Who is in the portrait? What time are they from? Are they male or female? If you are called to a memento, use your understanding of energy and vibration to recall this object and who it belonged to.

8.   Enter the photo, or the portrait. If you have a memento or object, hold onto it, and dissolve into it.

9.   You will find yourself immediately in a new surrounding: the photo, portrait, memento or object is a portal. It has transported you to somewhere else. This environment may be very different and unfamiliar to you: look around yourself, and notice everything.

10.   Look down, and notice your hands, your feet. Feel your hair. Are you man or woman? How old? Again, this particular body and personality may be very different than what you've experienced in this lifetime, or in previous regressions. Notice everything.

11.   Where are you drawn to go? To a building nearby? To a town in the distance? Something else? Go there now.

12.   You may be very unfamiliar with your surroundings, the people around you, and any events or situation you find yourself in. It is common to find yourself in situations where the energy is heightened, such as in the middle of a revolution, in a time of crisis, or another situation where the energy is very high.

13.   Recall that your guide has come with you. Ask your guide now, to help you understand why you are being shown

this lifetime. Ask what lessons you learned in this past life, and what you are to take with you in understanding.

14. If you sense that you are in danger, or even that this past life may show you your death, ask your guide to step in and shift this so you don't experience it. It is not harmful to experience this, but it may be uncomfortable or frightening. Simply ask your guide to remove you from the past life, if you sense this is happening.

15. When you are ready, you will easily find the portal to come back to the cavernous room. Go there. If there is any ceremony or ritual you are meant to do in this room, you will know that.

16. Begin to climb up the hallways through the root system, come out the tree trunk, and move your spirit self back into your body. Call your aura back to you, so that no parts of your soul energy are left in the past life, or anywhere else.

17. When you're ready, come back to this reality. Journal on what you experienced. If there was a lot of emotion in this past life, give yourself time and space to release it: take a shower or bath, get some food, take a walk, do normal grounding things.

For your journal

1. Who were you in this past life?

2. What did you do? What was your reality?

3. Were you in a heightened situation?

4. Did you experience danger or crisis?

5. What did you understand about this past life, and your soul lessons then?

Lesson 16

The River of Flow

The river as a portal to spiritual understanding comes up many times in many belief systems and mythologies. Most people relate the river to the idea of either the passage of a lifetime, such as from birth to death flowing over time, or as a way to look at what the environment is in a particular passage of a lifetime, or as a way to look at what's in the future—what's around the river bend. We can also use the river, or actually many rivers, as a technique in which we can jump time and jump lifetimes.

We're going to work with all of these.

First, what I have experienced is that the river is a portal to viewing the passage of a lifetime. We can view the river, and how we are on the river, as ways of showing us how we are in this lifetime. Let's look at this now.

The River of Flow

When you meditate and enter into the portal of the river, you enter into an environment that has all the characteristics of a regular river, but it is actually a river of energy. It is a spiritual river.

The river shows you different passages of time, depending on the guidance you are seeking. For example, the river can also show you passage of time, such as the weeks or months or year you are currently experiencing. The river can show you this lifetime—the passage of time from birth to death in this lifetime, as you flow down the river. The river can also show you infinite time—you literally float down the river, and you float from upstream to downstream, and the river never ends. It's a soul river, it's infinite, just as we are. And finally, the river can show you future times in future lifetimes.

To recap, you can work with the river to see:

- A small segment of time in this lifetime
- Your life to death in this lifetime
- The vast flow of infinite time, in all lifetimes
- Future lifetimes

Let's take a look at some of the symbolism the river uses, to help you navigate this experience.

Journeying the river

When entering the river portal, you'll want to notice several things. Of course, as with all journeying, anything can happen. This is just a list of what many people commonly experience doing this work.

Your boat

Sometimes you end up in a boat when you journey on the river—
sometimes you don't. You might find yourself on an inner tube,
raft, or in a canoe or kayak, or you might find yourself on a
tugboat, a sailboat, a huge yacht. Or you might be traveling on
nothing at all—you might be swimming or floating in the river
with no inner tube or boat at all.

Of course, the symbolism of what you find yourself traveling
on is one of the most important things to notice. If you are in a
tiny, leaky boat, this journey may be showing you difficulties in
your life. If you are on a huge yacht, that may point to prosperity
or support. If you are on a tugboat, that may point to the idea that
you are being towed forward or directed by others. The key is to
notice, and then to see what it means to you.

One recurrent vision I have when journeying on the river is of
myself standing on a raft, with a long pole to push myself forward.
The water is incredibly calm, it is the most beautiful setting, a very
wide river that seems to be in India. There are cows on the banks,
and people in robes, and large white birds in the air. My guides
are right with me, hovering over the water, encouraging me to go
forward. This vision shows me that I am supported on my spiritual
path, even when it feels that progress is painstakingly slow.

The current

The current refers to the speed at which things are moving. In
the example above, I was on a very slow, very calm river—there
was not much noticeable movement at all. This showed me that
things were happening, but slowly. However, sometime we find
ourselves in very fast, strong currents—this will tell you that
events are moving very quickly, and perhaps you are able to move
easily in the fast current, or perhaps it is too fast for you. If you
find yourself in very deep water, you may indeed be in over your
head, so to speak. If you find yourself in the shallows, you may
need to go deeper before you can go forward. If you find yourself

in incredibly stagnant, still or brackish water this might show you a place in which you are currently stuck. If the current is filled with rapids and high waves, you may have to use all your skills and strength to navigate.

The current is very easy to interpret. You will know what you need to understand as soon as you see it. As an example, if you found yourself in a giant yacht, but you had run aground because the water was very shallow, you might interpret this as having too expensive of tastes for your budget, or having too big of plans for what you can currently accomplish, or some other aspect of comparing big and small. If you found yourself on the muddy flats with no boat, just walking through quicksand, you would relate this to something going on in your life that was keeping you stuck. If you were in a rowboat and struggling with the current, you might be struggling with some aspects in your own life. And so on.

Dangers

When you face dangers in the water, such as big boulders in your way, crocodiles that slither off the banks, sharks or snakes or anything else sinister, it is a great time to ask this danger what it represents in your real life. Often a person, situation or event will come to mind immediately in relationship to this dangerous vision. If you aren't sure, ask the danger to tell you what it's about. If it is simply bad weather all around, this may point to a stormy time now or soon to come. If it's a specific danger, discover what it is so that you can carry this guidance back to your reality.

People

You may find yourself in a boat with someone, or riding in a boat being driven by someone else, or you might find there are people in other boats, or in the water, or on the bank of the river. These may be people you know, or people unknown to you. Once again, it's very easy to figure out. Simply notice who is there, and what the symbolism reminds you of. For example, if your river vision shows you riding in a boat that is captained by someone else, you might interpret this as being in a relationship where someone else is running the show. If you find there are crowds of people on the river bank waving to you, you might see this as welcoming and supportive energy from others. If you find someone flailing in the river, and you need to throw them a life raft, this may point to a relationship where you are saving others. And so on.

The river is a very interesting way to receive information from the Universe, because it is a meditation in which you will be so acutely aware of the environment around you—you will be on the river, feeling the current, feeling the wind, feeling the weather, the same way you would feel if you were on the river in real life. It is a very dynamic experience!

I find the best way to work with the river portal is to determine what passage of time you'd like to look at: a short passage, a longer passage, the infinite cycle of your life or a future time, and then simply enter the portal and see what is there for you to know.

For example, you might visit the river and ask "What's going on in my job over the next three months?" and you will receive that message. If you ask "What is my soul journey in this lifetime?" you will get an answer that spans from now until your death. If you ask "What is my soul journey in all lifetimes?" you may see glimpses of you as soul traveling in past lives, this life and future lives. So, in choosing the time frame you wish to look at, you can take a closer look or a broader look, depending on what you're most interested in. Or, you enter into the river portal many times, ask different questions, and receive all the information that you receive.

As you know, I am personally a big fan of very broad questions, such as "What is my destiny in this lifetime?" or "What is most important for me to know right now?" as it's my experience that these broad and open-ended questions help take us out of ego state and allow the Universe to provide information that we haven't even considered before.

Meditation: The River and Relationship

Here is the long form for journeying on the river. For this meditation, I'd like you to ask a simple question, such as "What is my relationship to X?" whether X is a relationship, a job, an experience, a situation—whatever in your life you have a question about right now. You'll be working in a near time frame, such as today to a year from now.

Let's try it now.

1.   Close your eyes.

2.   Breathe in through the nose, out through the mouth. Repeat this several times, until you feel very relaxed and possibly a little woozy.

3.   See yourself on the river. There is no need to arrive there in any particular way, you will just imagine the river in your mind, and you will know that you are there.

4.   A guide will arrive to accompany you. Notice if this is a "generic" guide or one you work with often. The guide may not be in the river with you, but will be watching from the bank or will be hovering in the air above or will be present in some other way.

5.   Pose your question in your mind, such as "What is my relationship to X?"

6.   Begin to notice how you're traveling. Are you in a boat, on a raft, in the water? Notice what method of transportation you have on the river. This method of transportation, whether you're on a fancy yacht or a broken raft, will be symbolic of how you are experiencing your relationship to X.

7.   Begin to notice the river itself. Is it a fast moving stream, flat shallows, is there a waterfall ahead? Are you in dangerous rapids, or are you in a burbling stream. The energy of the

river shows you time and energy that are symbolic of how you are experiencing your relationship to X.

8. Are there any obstacles in the water? Are there boulders, or other boats, or sharks, or anything else? Just notice whatever else is in the water, and see how it relates to your question.

9. Begin to notice if anyone else is with you. Who are they? What are they doing? How is this part of your answer?

10. Begin to notice what is happening on the banks of the river. Are there people there? Buildings? What else? What's happening there? How is this part of your answer?

11. If you're still not sure of your answer, or want further clarification, ask your guide to show you more clearly, or help you understand more easily. Notice what happens.

12. If you find yourself sailing down the river, just go with that. You may travel a short ways or a long ways, depending on what the Universe would like you to notice. You may be traveling from right to left (the most common), straight forward, or left to right. It's possible to travel another way, such as for a bird to arrive on your boat, and then you begin to travel with the bird. Just notice everything and contemplate how it relates to your question.

13. When you're ready to return to this reality, start counting yourself back from 10 to one. You don't need to use any particular bridge or tool to come back, just come back. When you're back in your body, open your eyes.

For your journal

1. What were you traveling on? What did this symbolize to you?

2. What was your river like? What did this mean to you?

3.   Who were you with? What else happened?

4.   What did you understand about this experience? How did the river answer your question "What is my relationship to X?"

Lesson 17

The River and Future Seeing

The river is also an excellent portal for viewing how things are unfolding in your life. You can do this as a whole life view, such as "Show me what my life looks like in the next 10 years?" or you can look at one aspect of your life, such as "Show me what my life's work or career looks like in the next 10 years?" or "Show me what my health looks like in the next 10 years?" or whatever you'd like to look at.

Of course, you can ask for a different time frame than 10 years. That is a useful length of time to work with, but you can adjust it to a year, 20 years, from now until death, or whatever you choose.

It would seem that this technique would also work if you wanted to look at what's unfolding for someone else's life, too. But does it? Yes, and no. In general, just as we can use the various journeying systems in this book to look at our own lives, we can use those to some degree to look at what's happening for our partner, family, friend, boss, or even our enemy. However, the Universe limits what we can see.

If a person asks you to journey on their behalf, you will be able to tell them what you see, and the Universe will provide you with the information that is yours to know. If you try to journey for someone else, you will likely not receive much information. If you journey with yourself in relationship to someone else, you will receive information about the relationship—the dance you and this other person are doing together.

Always, the Universe brings you back to the core questions about you:

- Why are you here?
- How are you doing?
- What is your mission or destiny?
- What soul lessons are you learning?
- What soul lessons are you resistant to learning?
- What signs and messages are you not noticing?
- Where is the flow of your life taking you?

Meditation: The River and Future Seeing

Here is the long form for journeying on the river for future seeing.

In this meditation, we're going to use the river as a portal to show us where the flow of your life is taking you. In other words, we will see a snapshot of where you are headed, with your current desires and actions. This is a destiny that you can continue to, or that you can adjust and shift, depending on how you like the vision that you see.

Let's try it now.

1.   Close your eyes.

2.   Breathe in through the nose, out through the mouth. Repeat this several times, until you feel very relaxed and possibly a little woozy.

3.   See yourself on the river. There is no need to arrive there in any particular way, you will just imagine the river in your mind, and you will know that you are there.

4.   A guide will arrive to accompany you. Notice if this is a generic guide or one you work with often. The guide may not be in the river with you, but will be watching from the bank or will be hovering in the air above or will be present in some other way.

5.   Pose your question in your mind, such as "How is my future unfolding?" or "What destiny am I moving toward?"

6.   Begin to notice how you're traveling. Are you in a boat, on a raft, in the water? Notice what method of transportation you have on the river. This method of transportation, whether you're on a fancy yacht or a broken raft, will be symbolic of how your future is unfolding.

7.   Begin to notice the river itself. Is it a fast moving stream, flat shallows, is there a waterfall ahead? Are you in dangerous rapids, or are you in a burbling stream. The energy of the river show you time and energy that are symbolic of how your future is unfolding.

8.   Are there any obstacles in the water? Are there boulders, or other boats, or sharks, or anything else? Just notice whatever else is in the water, and see how it relates to your question.

9.   Begin to notice if anyone else is with you. Who are they? What are they doing? How is this part of your answer?

10. Begin to notice what is happening on the banks of the river. Are there people there? Buildings? What else? What's happening there? How is this part of your answer?

11. Ask to become clear on what time frame you are being shown. Is this answer for this year, 10 years, until death? Just ask, and you'll have a sense of what time frame you're being shown.

12. If you're still not sure of your answer, or want further clarification, ask your guide to show you more clearly, or help you understand more easily. Notice what happens.

13. Stay with the meditation, and just allow anything else that needs to happen, whatever you need to notice, whatever you need to do. Just allow this as you receive further information.

14. When you're ready to return to this reality, start counting yourself back from 10 to one. You don't need to use any particular bridge or tool to come back, just come back. When you're back in your body, open your eyes.

For your journal

1. What were you traveling on? What did this symbolize to you?

2. What was your river like? What did this mean to you?

3. Who were you with? What else happened?

4. What did you understand about this experience? How did the river answer your question "How is my future unfolding?"

Part Seven

Dreams

Lesson 18

Unexpected Journeying

Dreaming is unexpected journeying. We can't control the process. We cannot intentionally decide in advance what we would like to dream, or what we will have revealed to us in a dream. And, this is a good thing!

Although I have read many books on lucid dreaming and set many intentions and done many experiments trying to control or influence what I would like to dream about, I have not had success at being able to choose what my dream would be each night.

Sometimes my dreams are incredibly real, more real than this life. Sometimes they show a recurring situation that I dream about repeatedly over many months or years. At times they are visionary dreams that show me my next step. Sometimes they are a jumble of experiences that don't make a lot of sense. Sometimes I don't remember my dreams. Sometimes my dreams are a series of deep answers that arrive one after the other, each answer more profound than the next.

I have flown in dreams, I have walked through walls in dreams, I have died in dreams, I have been to other realms and experienced many different beings and realities. And yet, I have still not mastered how to control the dreams that arrive.

And, I have come to understand that this is just fine.

In fact, it's how it's supposed to be.

It is not necessary to try to control or dictate what we dream. In fact, trying to control our dreams or wanting to have certain dreams isn't useful to us at all. After all, in all other approaches to psychic journeying—in all the ways we can journey in the Divine realms—we don't tell the Universe what needs to happen. In fact, of the most important aspects of direct connection with the Divine is that we are continually surprised by what the Universe shows us.

This is part of what makes direct connection so effective.

The Universe is continually communicating with us in ways that surprise us, and this is one of the ways we pay attention. If we could dictate what happened in meditation, we would not learn anything new. It would be a closed loop of our egoic brain, telling us what we want to hear. Nothing new in that loop. But when we let go of our need for egoic control, and simply allow the Universe to bring us what we need to know, we are able to live in a state of flow, living soul first.

So, if you've worked in lucid dreaming, I'd love for you to let go of any of those ideas of being able to control your dream, or control how you act or respond in a dream, and just allow the Universe to lead you into the dream experience that will be best for you.

The only thing we're going to ask the Universe is to bring us the exact dream experience we need. Just as we go into meditation without having any idea of what will be revealed to us, we're going to go to bed without having any idea of what we'll dream or what kind of dream we'll have. Our only intention will be that we are open to dreaming—we are fully willing to go into a dream journey with the Universe.

Dreaming meditations

We have all heard about how we sleep in different stages, and how we are likely to have different kinds of dreams at different times of the night or during different passages of our sleep. This is all interesting work.

However, my belief is that dreaming is a spiritual experience. It is a way that we allow ourselves to sink into a trance state, and we stay in this trance state for many hours at a time.

Within this perspective, you might think of sleeping as a very long meditation—we get settled into bed or wherever we will be resting, and then we drop out of this reality and into a different reality, and we may stay there for a seven or eight hours or longer.

It's curious to think about sleep as a meditation, isn't it? Because normally, we don't meditate for seven or eight hours in a row. We might find that difficult or even impossible to meditate that long. And yet, when we sleep we enter into a trance state, and we stay in that trance state without any difficulty, and during that time we journey into other dimensions.

In this way, we can consider sleep as a grand meditation we do every single night. It's a seven or eight-hour journey into the Divine realms! It's a dreaming meditation that we do as a practice, whether we intend to or not. When we understand that sleep— that dreams are actually spiritual journeying—we understand why sleep is such a magnificent spiritual practice.

What a gift to have sleep and dreams! What a gift to be able to go into a quiet space and simply connect with the Universe for seven or eight hours—and to be able to do this every day, for our whole lives. It is here that the Divine can reach us, and all we have to do is close our eyes.

Waking dreams

And sleep is not the only time this happens for us.

During much of the day—much of our waking hours—we are in waking dreams.

When we hold the intention to be fully present in as much of our lives as we can, we start to find that we are journeying not only when we sleep, but during waking hours too.

Spacing out, zoning out, day dreaming, flights of fancy—these are all negative words to describe this state of being in a waking dream. Yet, disassociating from reality in this kind of day-dreamy way is a not a negative thing! Rather, it is a connection to the Universe, a dropping into source that is incredibly healing and supportive.

It is also the main way we are able to access our intuition during our day-to-day activities.

You can choose to be in a reality that is lockstep with all the worry, fear and false news that we are bombarded with at every hour. Or you can lift off from that false narrative, and live in another reality—another dimension—entirely.

It's all about intention, really.

We can do the dishes hurriedly, just trying to get them done. Or we can let our mind go free when we do the dishes, and suddenly we are there in body but our souls are soaring around somewhere else—we've shifted to a different vibrational reality. We're doing the dishes in reverie.

We can sit in traffic, fuming that we're going to be late. Or we can find ourselves journeying to the most fantastic realms, even as we wait. We can journey to a different vibrational reality. We're sitting in grace, not traffic.

So, even in ordinary times, we're drifting in and out of meditation, or meditative states. We do this all day long. Any time you space out, day dream, zone out, imagine, are involved in an activity that takes you to flow—any time we move from the normal vibrational level of day-to-day living, into a heightened vibrational level of mindfulness, consciousness or reverie—we move into a state of waking dreams.

Again, this happens all day long.

Some people are more prone to drifting into these walking dreams, especially creative people, introverts, or all the sensitives reading this! But people who don't want to be in waking dreams go there, too. Even the person who is the most logical, linear, left-brain style person, also spends many hours of the waking life in a waking dream.

This is how we are designed: we are souls in human bodies, and the soul part can't be taken out of us. So, of course we are drifting out of our mind/ego/personality states and into our soul states all day and night. It's who we are!

We can accelerate this by holding intention to connect to the Universe during our waking hours—to agree to be a part of the waking dream. We can also choose certain activities that naturally bring on this state of diffuse connection. For example, when you are doing things like being in nature, listening to ambient or healing music, working on creative pursuits, reading uplifting work, then you are entering the waking dream. It also happens easily in exercise, or sex, or even when we are taking a shower—we are not trying to go into meditative reverie, and yet we do.

Living the dream

So, what happens when you're spending hours in dreaming meditation while you sleep, and more hours of waking dream when you are awake? Pretty soon, you're realizing that most or much of your life is spent living from your soul, not your mind.

Pretty soon, you can see that the hours and minutes add up. You can see that you're in this state of trance, this state of connection with the Divine, for many, many hours of the day. Even if you're not trying or don't want to try. You are continually drifting off to immerse yourself in the vibrational state of collective soul, of Universal flow.

We are always connected to the Divine/God/Universe/Oneness/Source.

We consciously connect, such as when we meditate.

We connect without trying, such as when we sleep.

We connect without realizing that's what's happening, such as when we drift into waking dream.

We connect when we do practices and activities that take us into flow state.

All of this is natural, normal, healthy, perfect! We are souls in human bodies, and we are here to live soul-led lives. In fact, there is not another way we can live. It is how we are designed, and it is who we are.

Lesson 19

Spiritual Dreaming

Now that we understand we're all walking around in a waking dream, let's go back to the bigger dreamtimes—the longer seven or eight-hour dreams that we have, when we go to sleep. In general, there are going to be several spiritual-dream styles you're going to experience. These include:

- Recurring dreams
- Prophetic dreams
- Visitation dreams
- Destiny dreams

All of these are wonderful ways to dream, and they happen naturally—you can't try to make then happen, they just do. If you are having any of these kinds of dreams, which we'll discuss soon, you can trust that you are open to the messages, signs and synchronicities of the Universe.

If you already dream a lot, you might begin to notice which of the spiritual dreams listed above that you most often have, and if there is a pattern that is starting to show up. Maybe you're receiving the same message over and over, or being visited by the same beings. Maybe something else is happening. Just receive it all as guidance, and notice the patterns.

If you don't dream much, don't remember your dreams, or don't think you've ever had a spiritual dream, you might ask the Universe to provide you with more vivid dreams, along with the ability to retain your dreams when you wake up. Again, you can't control what you will dream, but you can ask!

Many people like to keep a dream journal, and it's a great way to recall what you dream. Keep a journal by your bed, and as soon as you wake up—and before you get out of bed—jot down what you remember. It can be especially helpful to draw some rough sketches of what you recall, as sketching can sometimes capture meaning more quickly than language.

I also try to meditate upon my dreams as soon as I realize I am awake. The moment I realized I'm awake, I try not to move, I keep my eyes closed, and I try to reenter the dream for any last bits of wisdom. If I'm not able to reenter the dream, I will sit up—still in bed—and meditate. I will go into vastness, directly upon waking, and allow the dream and the meditation to merge and to provide whatever information is meant to be revealed. Sometimes I recall the dream, sometimes I receive messages, sometimes visions, sometimes I just want my coffee! But I give myself that time, so that the Universe is able to communicate if there is something more to be understood.

Spiritual dreams really deserve a book of their own! Since I haven't written that book yet, for now it's enough to be aware that the Universe is actively communicating with you every time you sleep, and the dreams you receive can provide extraordinary guidance for you on your soul path.

Now let's take a look at spiritual dreams in a little more depth.

Recurring dreams

Recurring dreams are dreams in which we're working out a soul lesson. We may have the same recurring dream for our entire life, or we may have the same recurring dream for many years of our lives. For example, as a child I had a recurring dream that a cowboy would come and shoot at my feet while telling me to dance faster. This was obviously a nightmare! Now, it's easy to say I must have had some experience that brought me to that dream—seen something on TV, perhaps.

This dream might point to some kind of anxiety—of needing to dance or please people so that I would not get punished. I was a very sensitive, anxious child, so this makes sense to me.

However, many recurring dreams are past lives. They are times when our past lives come back to us, and we are revisiting an event we have not fully processed. Viewing your recurring dreams in this way, as a past-life experience or past-life lesson you have not processed or integrated, can be helpful.

More recently, for the past decade I've had a recurring dream that involves packing suitcases for my family members. Sometimes I am packing my children's suitcases, and as I put the clothing in, it all falls out. I am trying to get my family all packed up and to the airport, and time is running out. Sometimes my ex-husband is in this dream, sometimes my departed father is in this dream. Sometimes I am in the house I grew up in, sometimes I don't know where I am. There are always the suitcases that won't get packed, or if they do get packed, they fall open or burst at the seams or some other disaster. So, we never can get to the airport.

Until—one day—the dream changed. In the dream, the suitcases were still not packing correctly, but I got to the airport with everything in tow. From that dream on, I did not have that recurring dream again.

I began instead to have a very confusing dream about traveling in a town or city where there is water everywhere. Not in a problematic way, but in a way the city is designed: there are roadways that go over water, and there are many canals everywhere.

It is a city intentionally built on water. I am driving various family members, and there is no problem in this dream, except we don't know where we are going. We need to get somewhere, but we don't know where.

This dream is recurring because I am working on a soul lesson of feeling lost, or feeling that I am not sure where I am going, or even where I should be trying to go. The Universe is bringing this to my attention, so that I will notice it. I would expect over time that this dream will also change.

If you have recurring dreams, the best thing to do is notice how long you've had them, what they refer to, and what they are asking you to pay attention to.

You'll notice I don't head to a dream dictionary, in order to get my meaning! I trust that just as when we receive guided visions, we have the ability to understand clearly that feeling, emotion and overall message of the dream. We are souls, and we do not need dream dictionaries to interpret everything! We can just unpack the dream, look at it, and open to the awareness that it is bringing.

Prophetic dreams

Prophetic dreams are dreams that show us the future in real life. This can be about something in your personal life, such as foreseeing an event that comes to pass. Or they can be about something that affects the soul collective, such as a natural disaster or big event.

Many people receive a great deal of information about the future in their dreams. Usually, a prophetic dream will show you a movie of what will happen in the future, and then you will later—usually within days or weeks—see that future come to pass.

I do not usually have prophetic dreams, but I did have a prophetic dream about the Japanese tsunami, which came to pass a few days after my dream. I saw the tsunami as a movie in my dreams, and then later when I was watching the news feeds, there was a clear sense of déjà vu—I dreamt this!

Many people had prophetic dreams of the twin towers coming down, or of earthquakes, or the onslaught of forest fires, and so on. This can be very distressing, of course, but I find refuge in the reality that we are not able to control the world or all aspects of our destiny, and that we are infinite souls. What will happen happens. There is no sense having anxiety over anything until it arrives at your door, and even then, we can choose to respond without fear, trusting our infinite nature.

If you are a person who has a lot of prophetic dreams, and you find these disturbing, you can ask the Universe to dial these down for you. You can simply go into meditation, and ask the Universe to stop sending you prophetic dreams about your family, or about the world. They will become fewer, you won't remember them as much, and you won't be distressed about them.

On the other hand, if you have a spiritual outlook that allows you to receive these dreams with equanimity, you can ask the Universe to dial these up for you. Foreseeing the future may be useful to you or to others.

Visitation dreams

Visitation dreams are dreams where we are visited by other beings. This could be the departed, a person who is living now, or a guide or an angel. For example, many people have dreams about their departed loved ones, and these dreams are so vivid, it is impossible to think they are only dreams. Many people have woken up to see a beloved departed standing by their bed—their grandmother, or someone else they know and love. These dreams are meant as signs of support—they are messages of love and light, from the other side.

While I rarely have visitation dreams, several years ago I had a vivid dream of my departed father—he died about 20 years ago. In the dream, he entered the room and sat down at the end of the bed. I saw the door open, I saw him come in, I felt the pressure of someone sitting on the bed, and I was aware of myself sitting up, and of my husband sleeping beside me. It was so incredibly real! I just looked at my dad, me sitting up in bed and he sitting on the edge of the bed, He was shimmering, or glowing, and he looked much younger than when he passed. I did not receive a message from, just the deep awareness of his presence. When I woke up in the morning, I could not believe he had not physically been there.

Other times, visitation dreams involve a person who is living— you have dream that is so vivid, that involves you interacting, conversing or going on a journey with a person you know. What is interesting here, is that these people may not be currently all that important in your real life. For example, you might dream about a childhood friend you've lost contact with, a man you dated decades ago and haven't talked to sense, someone else not actively in your life. These dreams show unfinished business, usually on a karmic level. You do not need to contact this person, unless you are drawn to. Unfinished business on a karmic level means you have past-life karma with this person, and the Universe is reminding you of your deeper connection over many lifetimes.

If you have a visitation dream about someone you've long forgotten, simply fold it in with all of the other mysteries in the Universe. Notice it, and be aware of what else may or may not show up surround this person. Sometimes there's something, sometimes we don't know.

Destiny dreams

Destiny dreams show us a vision of our life's calling. You may have a destiny dream only once in your life, or at most a few times. Destiny dreams happen when we are ready to start a new chapter in our life—to begin new work, to move to a new part of the world, to begin a new partnership, or to drop our past and begin life as a new person. These are dreams that show big shifts—life-altering changes that mean we are stepping form one reality into another. In destiny dreams, we are shown why we are truly here— the work we are here to do, the people we are here to work with, the places we are meant to inhabit.

Destiny dreams especially occur during the pivotal passages in our life: in our early 20s, at our first Saturn return at 28, in our early 40s, in our late 50s at our second Saturn return, in the early 70s, and at the mid-80s. Each time, we are invited to understand the true meaning of why we are here. We are invited to shift course if we have strayed from our soul's destiny, and to step forward without fear if we are shown a new path.

I was not aware of any destiny dreams in my early twenties or first Saturn return, although I made great shifts in my life them— starting a first career path in my early twenties, and moving to a different town away from my birth family, along with starting a family of my own at my first Saturn return. I wasn't very aware of my dreams then, or perhaps I wasn't paying attention. I wasn't very aware at that time of my life—I had not yet woken up.

By my early 40s, which was the time of my near death experience and psychic awakening, I was well attuned to my dreams. I dreamt frequently of a strange kind of house in the woods—it had a driveway, and it had a certain kind of ceiling that was very strange—very high and partly open. Soon after I moved into this house, where I would live for the next 15 years. The moment I saw it, I recognized the carport in front of the house as the "ceiling" in my dreams. This house was a soul's destiny for me, as living in the country was a great teacher to me—in fact, my opening awareness of nature changed my life.

If you receive a destiny dream, please treasure it. It is a gift from the Universe. Please also follow it, as completely and quickly as you are able. These dreams are rare, and only come a few times during a lifetime. They are meant to provide you with clear guidance and direction. If you follow them, you will be taken on a new path—you will be shown the destiny you are here to fulfill in this lifetime.

For your journal

1.   Have you had a recurring dream when you were young? What was it, and what did it mean to you then?

2.   Do you have recurring dreams now? What does your dream mean to you?

3. Have you had prophetic dreams that foretold the future? What were they, and what happened?

4. Have you had visitation dreams from other beings? What happened?

5. Have you had a destiny dream in your life? Write what you remember about it now.

Epilogue

Collective Soul

Lesson 20

Oneness

As you've worked through the concepts and exercises we've been covering, I am certain that you've had extraordinary experiences.

The thing to remember as you do all this work, much of it in a state of wonder or even disbelief, as in "How could I have seen that?" or "What a strange journey I have taken!" is that none of this is new for your soul.

The portals of spiritual journeying—all the places we have been in this practice—are where your soul lives.

Your soul doesn't actually hang out in your head or at the top of your head like some tethered halo. It is a consciousness that is always connecting to all the realms, all the portals, all dimensions, all the time. You can call it your soul into your body—by becoming still, by becoming present—and, in this way, you will remember your true self.

But also true, even as you sense your soul within your self and as your true infinite essence, is that your soul is everywhere, always, and it is not alone. You and I and everyone and everything are all part of collective soul, which is the same and not different from God/Universe/One/All/Divine. It is the same as your guides and angels, which are expressions or translators for Source.

There are so many ways to be in the Universe, and this is all you. And me. And every thing. Every little aspect of everything affects everything else in this dance of infinite connection forever.

The reward of your own spiritual journeying has been soul awakening—seeing things that you have not seen before, and bringing that understanding back to your human life. So, spiritual journeying has been rewarding for you—it has helped you increase your consciousness on the path of soul growth for you. And yet, it has also been beneficial to others.

When you remember that you are part of collective soul, indivisible and never separate, it is clear that what affects one affects all. Thus, when you meditate, when you journey, when you connect to the Universe, when you heal, when you expand, it is not just happening for you. It is happening for all souls, as part of collective soul.

Spread the word of these practices. Talk about your journeying. Share with others. As you continue your practice of exploring all the layers and levels of the Universe, which is also you, you not only lift up yourself but you lift up collective soul. In this way the whole Universe, which is you and you and you and everyone and everything, continues its expansion into Light.

We are all in this together. The more you connect to Light, the more collective soul is also connected to Light. Do you see how this is the way that you and the Universe evolve? Whenever you do your spiritual practice, your meditation, your journeying, your listening, your opening, the whole Universe is expanded at the same time.

Thank you for doing your spiritual practice, for your soul journeying. If you have always wanted to help others, to help the world, you are.

The more you know yourself as soul, the more you lift collective soul. Over time, with your connection and with the connection of others, consciousness expands. Over time, which happens in all dimensions all at once, we grown in our awareness of ourselves as One.

About the Author

Sara Wiseman is a visionary spiritual teacher and award-winning author who has taught tens of thousands of students worldwide via her many books, courses and training. She is the author of:

- *Messages from the Divine: Wisdom for the Seeker's Soul*
- *Writing the Divine: How to Use Channeling for Soul Growth & Healing*
- *Your Psychic Child: How to Raise Intuitive & Spiritually Gifted Kids of All Ages*
- *The Intuitive Path: The Seeker's Guide to Spiritual Intuition*
- *Living a Life of Gratitude: Your Journey to Grace, Joy & Healing*
- *The Four Passages of the Heart: Moving from Pain into Love*
- *Intuition, Cancer & Miracles: A Passage of Hope and Healing*
- *Daily Divine: Inspirations for a Soul-Led Life, Book One*
- *Daily Divine: Inspirations for a Soul-Led Life, Book Two*
- *Mystic, Lover, Seeker, Saint: The Four Paths of Spiritual Awakening*
- *Connect with Your Loved Ones in Spirit: How to Contact Family & Friends Who've Crossed Over*

Sara is the founder of *Intuition University*, writes the award-winning *Daily Divine* blog, hosts the *Ask Sara* and *Spiritual Psychic* podcasts, is the creator of *Divine Oracle*, and has released four healing CDs with her band Martyrs of Sound. She lives in Oregon with her family.

Connect with Sara at

www.sarawiseman.com

For more information about
Sara Wiseman's work in spirituality and intuition,

please visit www.sarawiseman.com